PRESENTED TO

_____

BY

_____

OCCASION

_____

fP

Become a
Better
You

JOURNAL

A Guide to
Improving Your Life
Every Day

JOEL OSTEEN

FREE PRESS
New York London Toronto Sydney

FREE PRESS

A Division of Simon & Schuster, Inc.
1230 Avenue of the Americas
New York, NY 10020

First Free Press hardcover edition April 2008

FREE PRESS and colophon are trademarks of Simon & Schuster, Inc.

For information about special discounts for bulk purchases,
please contact Simon & Schuster Special Sales at 1-800-456-6798
or business@simonandschuster.com.

Manufactured in the United States of America

1   3   5   7   9   10   8   6   4   2

Library of Congress Cataloging-in-Publication Data

Osteen, Joel.
Become a better you journal : a guide to living at your full potential / by Joel Osteen.
p. cm.
1. Self-actualization (Psychology)—Religious aspects—Christianity.
2. Christian life. I. Title.
BV4598.2.O86 2008
248.4—dc22   2008007115

ISBN-13: 978-1-4165-7306-7
ISBN-10:   1-4165-7306-2

CONTENTS

Introduction   xi

STEP ONE:
KEEP PRESSING FORWARD

Day 1:   Tap Into God's Gifting   3

Day 2:   Good Soil for Growing   7

Day 3:   The Champion Within   11

Day 4:   It's in Your Blood   15

Day 5:   The Impossible Dream   19

Day 6:   A Lasting Legacy   23

Day 7:   Divine Destiny   27

STEP TWO:
BE POSITIVE TOWARD YOURSELF

Day 1:   A Good Listener   33

Day 2:   Just as You Are   37

Day 3:   Letting Go and Holding On   41

Day 4:   Your Own Best Friend   45

Day 5:   Words of Love   49

Day 6:   Thoughts of Affirmation   53

Day 7:   The New Self   57

STEP THREE:
DEVELOP BETTER RELATIONSHIPS

Day 1: Giving Back 63

Day 2: People Investments 67

Day 3: A Blanket of Love 71

Day 4: Blessed Are the Peacemakers 75

Day 5: Family Ties That Bind 79

Day 6: Better to Give 83

Day 7: God's Delegate 87

STEP FOUR:
FORM BETTER HABITS

Day 1: Feeding the Good Wolf 93

Day 2: Whatever Is Noble 97

Day 3: Living Joy 101

Day 4: God in Your View 105

Day 5: A Well of Good Things 109

Day 6: Run the Race 113

Day 7: Responsible Happiness 117

STEP FIVE:
EMBRACE THE PLACE WHERE YOU ARE

Day 1: Faith Teaches 123

Day 2: Resting in Trust 127

Day 3: Joyful in Hope 131

Day 4: The Gift of Memory 135

Day 5: Talking to Yourself 139

Day 6: Backstage Miracles 143

Day 7: God in the Details 147

STEP SIX:
DEVELOP YOUR INNER LIFE

Day 1:   The Still, Small Voice   153

Day 2:   A Step at a Time   157

Day 3:   A Tender Conscience   161

Day 4:   Trust and Obey   165

Day 5:   The Clean Slate   169

Day 6:   Digging Deep   173

Day 7:   No Pain, No Gain   177

STEP SEVEN:
STAY PASSIONATE ABOUT LIFE

Day 1:   Providing for Abundance   183

Day 2:   A Song in Your Heart   187

Day 3:   Hope Is a Smile   191

Day 4:   Plan for Success   195

Day 5:   Say No to No   199

Day 6:   Fanning the Flame   203

Day 7:   Willing What's Right   207

INTRODUCTION

Many people today are discovering the priceless seeds of greatness that God has placed within them. They are stretching forward with a vision for who God intends them to be—a better version of themselves, a person living at the highest level.

How do you become a better you? The answer is simple. You become a better you when you stop settling for mediocrity in your thoughts, attitudes, or actions, and focus instead on the you God has in mind. You dig deep to discover what is holding you back, then reach ahead to the image of God in you and the blessings He is waiting to pour into your life.

You, too, can discover these seeds of greatness, and this book will help you do it.

Become a Better You Journal is made up of seven parts, one for each principle in my bestselling book *Become a Better You*. Each part is divided into seven days' worth of material for you to consider, so this should take you seven weeks to get through. Resist the temptation to read the whole book at once, and really take your time to digest each piece. Make each day an opportunity for reflection. As you make your way through the next seven weeks, the principles will become increasingly clear to you. You might find it helpful to read the original book, but you can use this journal without it. I'll remind you of the material in the main book by including brief summaries that we can use as launching places.

That's what the journal is all about—thought and reflection. It's an invitation for you to reach new levels of self-discovery so you can stretch forward into the person you are meant to be. The journey you will take is an inner one that leads into your head, your heart, and your soul. As you go, though, you will see how profoundly the inner journey influences your outer walk. What you do in this journal, with God's blessing and guidance, will help you find better quality relationships, more productive use of your gifts and talents, and a more fulfilled life.

Trust God to walk beside you as you grow, learn, and improve. He will expand your vision, and you will become a better you!

HOW TO USE THIS BOOK

This book is yours to be *used*. It's your journal, designed to involve you more deeply in your experience of becoming a better you. Write in it, jot down thoughts in the margins, underline important ideas. It's yours to fill up with the insights and encouragements that come to you as you consider who you are, who God is, and the exciting opportunities you are discovering because of your relationship with Him.

In the pages to come, you'll find relevant Scriptures, stimulating questions, and seed prayers to help you focus your mind and heart on digging deeper into becoming the person God has planned for you to be. As you read, you'll also find ample space to write out your responses to the ideas and inspiration offered here. This book is not meant to be read in a couple of sittings. It is designed to give you seven weeks of daily reading, reflection, and encouragement. Give yourself the gift of time to ponder the questions. Let the Scriptures seep in and shape your soul. Listen for the still, small voice of God's grace and direction. Then put words to your responses.

It's possible, of course, to simply read and think. But writing your answers down forces you to nail down thoughts and feelings that might otherwise drift with distractions and competing concerns. Writing out your answers makes you really consider your behaviors and beliefs. Best of all, it gives you a record of your responses as God speaks to you in your time of study and meditation. You can come back to these pages again and again, to be refreshed, to reflect further on what you're seeing, and to be encouraged in your stretch toward God's fullest blessings. The world offers little "down" time for the deepest, most important business of your life—becoming the best person you can be. This journal can be your antidote to the hustle and noise that otherwise surround you.

As you write, put aside any worries about the mechanics of writing. You don't have to be a poet or a grammar expert. You don't have to spell everything correctly. You will have genuine feelings, beliefs, and ideas that need expression, and no one but you ever has to see the way you express them. There are no right or wrong answers to the questions on the pages to come. There are only *your* answers. Commit yourself to honesty and be as specific as you can, and God will richly bless you to change and grow.

If you want to make the most of your experience, I suggest that you set aside a block of time in a quiet, comfortable space where you can have some privacy. Express yourself fully, freely, and honestly. Anything less will rob you of the benefits and blessings available to you as you dedicate yourself to hearing God's voice. Especially seek God's help and guidance to see areas in which He wants you to grow and mature.

Let this journal be a testimony of your faith. Let it be a record of how God's work in your heart and mind is helping you to become a better you!

—Joel Osteen

STEP ONE

Keep Pressing Forward

DAY 1

TAP INTO GOD'S GIFTING

KEY TRUTH: God has gifted you to grow.

Neurologists have discovered that the average person uses less than 10 percent of his or her mind. That means more than 90 percent of the mind's capability lies dormant. It never gets tapped into. But if we could just understand what we have: God has deposited a part of Himself in you. When it came time for you to be born, God said, "Let Me give you some of this gift; some of this talent; some of this creativity." You have the seed of Almighty God inside you. You were never created to be average. You were never created to reach a certain level and then plateau. You were created to excel. There's no limit to how high you can go in life. There's no limit to what you can accomplish, if you will just learn to shake off complacency and keep stretching to the next level.

Maybe you've tried to succeed but have hit a brick wall again and again. Try again. If you've been told no a thousand times, ask again. Keep asking until you get the yes that you've been waiting to hear. Too many people grow satisfied with far less than God's best for their lives. Sometimes they get discouraged, but all too often, they simply get comfortable. They stop stretching; they are not exercising their faith; and like a once muscular, toned body that no longer exercises, they grow flabby.

Our potential has been put in us by our Manufacturer, our Creator, Almighty God. Whether we use it or not does not diminish it, but it does impact our future. The events of your past do not reduce your potential. How somebody has treated you or what they said about you doesn't change your potential. Maybe you've had some unfair things happen in life. None of that affects your potential.

CONSIDER THIS: God would not have put your dream in your heart if He had not already given you everything you need to fulfill it. That means that you don't have to worry whether you have what it takes to see that dream fulfilled. The key to rising higher is to keep looking to where you want to go. Dream big dreams! Don't focus on where you are today; keep a positive vision and see yourself accomplishing your goals and fulfilling your destiny. In the space provided below, reflect on your biggest dream. Write it out in detail. Record the first, second, and third steps you need to take to begin to stretch toward that dream.

Ideas are like rabbits.
You get a couple and learn how
to handle them, and pretty soon
you have a dozen.

—*John Steinbeck*

_____

_____

_____

_____

_____

_____

_____

_____

_____

_____

_____

—❦—

Nothing ever built arose to touch the skies unless some man dreamed that it should, some man believed that it could, and some man willed that it must.

—*Charles F. Kettering*

_____

_____

WHAT THE SCRIPTURES SAY

The LORD will guide you always;
he will satisfy your needs in a sun-scorched land
and will strengthen your frame.
You will be like a well-watered garden,
like a spring whose waters never fail.

—*Isaiah 58:11*

I thank my God every time I remember you. In all my prayers for all of you, I always pray with joy because of your partnership in the gospel from the first day until now, being confident of this, that he that began a good work in you will carry it on to completion until the day of Christ Jesus.

—*Philippians 1:3–6*

A PRAYER FOR TODAY

Lord, I believe that you have matched me with my world. You have planted the seed of your greatness in me and gifted me to fulfill the dreams you have placed in my heart. Please help me believe and have the courage to take hold of these dreams. I praise you in advance for the dreams that you will turn into reality.

_____

_____

_____

_____

_____

_____

_____

_____

_____

_____

_____

_____

_____

_____

TAKEAWAY TRUTH: My potential has been put in me permanently by the Creator of the Universe. When I believe, I take a step of faith and stretch myself; that's when I start to tap into God's gifting.

DAY 2

GOOD SOIL FOR GROWING

KEY TRUTH: An important key to reaching your full potential is putting yourself in an environment where the seed can grow.

The dream in your heart may be bigger than the environment in which you find yourself. Sometimes you have to get out of that environment in order to see that dream fulfilled.

Consider an oak tree. If you plant it in a pot, its growth will be limited. Once its roots fill that pot, it can grow no further. The problem is not with the tree; it is with the environment. It is stifling growth. Perhaps you have bigger things in your heart than your present environment can facilitate. That's why, at times, God will stir you out of a comfortable situation. When you go through persecution and rejection, it's not always because somebody has it in for you. Sometimes, that's God's way of directing you into His perfect will. He's trying to get you to stretch to the next level. He knows you're not going to go without a push, so He'll make it uncomfortable for you to stay where you are currently. The mistake we make at times is getting negative and sour; we focus on what didn't work out. When we do that, we inhibit the opening of new doors.

When one door closes, if you keep the right attitude, God will open another door. But you have to do your part and keep pressing forward. Let your hurt go. You may not understand it, but trust God and move on with your life. Don't look at it as the end. Look at it as a new beginning, knowing this: God accepts you. God approves you. And He has something better in store.

Throughout life, we're not always going to understand everything that happens along the way. But we've got to learn to trust God. We've got to believe that He has us in the palm of His hand, that He is leading and guiding us, that He always has our best interests at heart. Too many people get bitter, they get angry, and they start to blame God. Friend, don't die with the treasure still inside you. Keep pressing forward. Keep reaching for new heights. Give birth to what God has placed in your heart.

CONSIDER THIS: You may discover that, sometimes, if you don't keep things stirred up, God will stir things for you. When somebody leaves your life or a relationship is over, don't try to talk them into staying. Let God do a new thing. Create a positive environment. Find somebody happy to cheer you up. Get around people who will inspire you to rise higher. In the space below, write down three things that have disappointed you to the point that you were tempted to see them as the end, instead of as closed doors that could lead to other open ones. Then describe the new thing that God did or the new thing you can imagine God doing because you were shaken out of your routine.

_____

_____

_____

_____

_____

_____

_____

_____

_____

_____

_____

_____

_____

_____

_____

_____

_____

_____

Ah, great it is to believe the
dream as we stand in youth by
the starry stream; but a greater
thing is to fight life through and
say at the end, the dream is true!

—*Edwin Markham*

WHAT THE SCRIPTURES SAY

But blessed is the man who trusts in the LORD,
whose confidence is in him.
He will be like a tree planted by the water
that sends out its roots by the stream.
It does not fear when heat comes;
its leaves are always green. It has no worries in a year of drought
and never fails to bear fruit.

—*Jeremiah 17:7–8*

If you remain in me and my words remain in you, ask whatever
you wish, and it will be given you. This is to my Father's glory,
that you bear much fruit, showing yourselves to be my disciples.

—*John 15:7–8*

A PRAYER FOR TODAY

Father, I am putting my trust in you. You have called me to a time of new beginning, and I'm ready to get my fire and my passion back. I thank You for Your love and Your promise that I can rise out of my own past to grow and stretch into the future You have for me. I pray that You'll make me wise in my choice of human companions. Thank You for always being here with me.

_____

_____

_____

_____

A true friend never gets
in your way unless you
happen to be going down.

—*Arnold H. Glasow*

_____

_____

TAKEAWAY TRUTH: I have a responsibility to keep myself healthy and whole. I have a gift. God has entrusted me with it. I won't look back; I'll keep looking forward and getting ready for the new thing God wants to do in my life.

DAY 3

THE CHAMPION WITHIN

KEY TRUTH: You come from a bloodline of champions, and the champion within you is waiting to be discovered.

Have you ever noticed a champion racehorse, the kind you might see at the Kentucky Derby or another prestigious horse race? Those Thoroughbreds often have generation after generation of winners in their blood.

When that colt is first born, however, it may not look like much. His legs may be wobbly, he may not be able to stand up, and he may not be all that attractive. But the owners don't get worried or discouraged. They don't say, "Oh, no; this horse is a reject. He's not a Thoroughbred; look at him! His legs are too small. His stride is too short. His body is not strong and muscular." No, those owners know that in his blood, that colt carries a legacy of championship-winning genes. He's a winner in the making.

That's how you need to see yourself. You may have some flaws or weaknesses. You may not be the most beautiful or the most talented or the most intelligent, but that's okay. In your bloodline, you come from a long line of champions. You may not realize it right now, but your DNA is filled with strength, courage, ability, favor, and determination. You are full of can-do power. It doesn't matter what your current condition looks like. You may have some addictions or insecurities; you may not think you have what it takes to succeed, but that doesn't change what God put within you. You are the seed of Almighty God; the Psalmist said, "You have been fearfully and wonderfully made." Start seeing yourself as God sees you—as His child, strong, empowered, and filled with possibilities.

Winning is in the blood. God has already crowned you a champion.

CONSIDER THIS: Your Heavenly Father spoke the galaxies into existence. Your elder brother defeated the enemy. Moses parted the Red Sea. David, a shepherd boy, defeated Goliath with only a few pebbles. Samson toppled a building. Daniel spent an entire night in a lion's den and wasn't harmed. Nehemiah rebuilt the walls of Jerusalem when all the odds were against him. In your bloodline, there's great faith, courage, supernatural strength, divine protection, determination, and persistence. That's why you must quit focusing on your weaknesses and get a bigger vision for your life. Imagine a Bible passage that describes *you* in the lineage of champions. What might it say if you shed your doubts and let the person God created shine through? Write a realistic description, but one that reflects what God says about you.

_____

_____

_____

_____   ❦

_____   What counts is not necessarily
                         the size of the dog in the fight—
_____   it's the size of the fight
                         in the dog.
_____
                         —*President*
_____   *Dwight D. Eisenhower*

_____

_____   _____

_____

_____

_____

WHAT THE SCRIPTURES SAY

For you did not receive a spirit that makes you a slave again to fear, but you received the Spirit of sonship. And by him we cry, *Abba*, Father. The Spirit himself testifies with our spirit that we are God's children.

—*Romans 8:15–16*

Those who have faith are blessed with Abraham, the man of faith.

—*Galatians 3:9*

A PRAYER FOR TODAY

Lord, I know You have removed my chains. I know You have paid the price. You have put the blood of champions in my veins because You don't intend for my life to be mediocre. I thank You for giving me power over my enemies. I praise You for replacing the spirit of fear in me with the Spirit of sonship. You are in me, and You are greater than he that is in the world.

God asks no man whether
he will accept life. That is not
the choice. One must take it.
The only choice is how.

—*Henry Ward Beecher*

TAKEAWAY TRUTH: God has programmed me with everything I need for victory. I have what it takes. I am more than a conqueror. I am intelligent; I am talented; I am successful; I am attractive; I am an overcomer.

DAY 4

IT'S IN YOUR BLOOD

KEY TRUTH: You can break free from the strongholds of your past.

Where I grew up, folks often described a troublemaker by saying, "Well, he's just got bad blood." Really, there's some truth to that. What's in our bloodline is extremely important. We all have a natural bloodline flowing from our parents, grandparents, great-grandparents, and other members of our family tree.

Understand that we also have a spiritual bloodline. God planned everything and prearranged for you to be here at this particular time in history. Your value is not based on how somebody else has treated you or on how perfect of a life you have lived, or even on how successful you are. Your value is based solely on the fact that you are a child of God. No, you're not perfect. You make mistakes. You have weaknesses. That doesn't change your value in God's eyes. You are still the apple of His eye. You are still His most prized possession.

Sometimes "religion" tries to beat people down and make them feel bad about themselves. "You've done this and you failed here, and you didn't treat this person right, and you didn't raise your kids as well as you should have." But God knew you weren't going to be perfect. Why don't you lighten up and give yourself a break? You can't change the past. If you've made mistakes, just say, "God, I'm sorry; I repent. Help me to do better next time." Then let it go and move on.

Friend, you've got to believe in yourself and believe that you have something to offer this world that nobody else has. You've been made in the image of Almighty God. You are a person of destiny. You didn't just show up. God was thinking about you before you were even born.

CONSIDER THIS: God designed you as you are on purpose. You are an original. Quit being negative and critical toward yourself and start enjoying yourself as a unique creation of God. No matter how many mistakes you've made, you need to know that on the inside, you have the seed of Almighty God. You should go out each day expecting good things, anticipating God's blessings and favor. God has planned all of your days for good, not evil.

Use the space below to write out your negative thoughts and self-doubts. Describe them and how they make you feel about yourself. Then reflect on the Scripture passages that follow and describe the reality of who you are in God's loving, forgiving eyes.

_____

_____

_____

_____

_____

_____

_____

_____

_____

_____

_____

_____

_____   ———————❦———————

_____

_____   Mistakes are the usual
                                                   bridge between inexperience
_____   and wisdom.

_____   *—Phyllis Theroux*

_____

_____

_____

_____

_____

_____

_____

WHAT THE SCRIPTURES SAY

> Instead of their shame,
> my people will receive a double portion,
> and instead of disgrace
> they will rejoice in their inheritance.
>
> *—Isaiah 61:7*

Therefore, if anyone is in Christ, he is a new creation; the old has gone, the new has come!

> *—2 Corinthians 5:17*

A PRAYER FOR TODAY

Lord, I am sorry for my mistakes. I repent of my wrongdoing. I thank You for Your promise of forgiveness. I praise You for Your mercy toward me. Strengthen me to go forward and help me to know and do better in the future. Help me live like the child of God that You have made me.

_____

_____

_____

⁂

There is no saint without a past—
no sinner without a future.

—*ancient Persian mass*

_____

_____

_____

_____

_____

_____

_____

_____

TAKEAWAY TRUTH: God is waiting for me to rise up in my authority, to have a little backbone and determination. I am not going to live my life in mediocrity, bound by addictions, negative and defeated. I'm going to start pressing forward. I'm going to take hold of everything God has in store for me.

DAY 5

THE IMPOSSIBLE DREAM

KEY TRUTH: You can choose the blessing instead of the curse, and be the one that puts a stop to negative patterns, habits, and attitudes you inherited from generations before you.

Stephen and Susan's son Bradley started first grade, and he was so excited about it. He was outgoing and energetic and met many new friends. After a couple of months, however, Bradley began having intense panic attacks at school. He would get so upset and become afraid that his parents weren't going to come back and pick him up. Nothing his parents said calmed Bradley. Time after time, the parents would have to rush to the school and assure their child that everything was okay.

There was no reason for Bradley's unexplainable fear. Stephen and Susan were loving parents, and they had never before left him anyplace. Nevertheless, the panic attacks continued month after month. The situation got so bad that when Bradley was at home, he would not leave Susan's side. The couple was frustrated and heartbroken, wondering what they had done to cause this awful condition, and what they could do to help Bradley.

Then one day Stephen was talking with his father, the child's grandfather, and as he explained the situation, it was as though a light turned on in the grandfather's mind. "Stephen, I know exactly what's wrong with Bradley," the grandfather said. "When I was a little boy in the first grade, my father died suddenly. I was so afraid that when my mother would try to walk me to school, I would cry so hard, thinking that she might not come back. Many times she would just turn around and take me back home. I believe that somehow Bradley's fear is connected to mine." Stephen and Susan began to pray; daily they bound the stronghold of fear in their family's line, and they stood against that curse. Today, Bradley is a young man and is living a normal, healthy life.

CONSIDER THIS: Understand, if you are struggling with one or more of these negative patterns in your family's past, it does not make you a bad person. Somebody else made the poor choices, and now you have to deal with the repercussions. Don't use that as an excuse to perpetuate negative lifestyle patterns. You have to dig your heels in and do something about it.

Take one of the first steps to overcoming your generational curses by identifying them here. Admit your weaknesses. It is not easy, but it is necessary and it is liberating. Make a list here, and remember as you do that no negative pattern is too difficult for God. After each weakness you record, commit yourself to choosing to change and write: ALL THINGS ARE POSSIBLE WITH GOD.

_____

_____

_____

_____

_____

_____

_____

_____

_____

_____

_____

_____   —❧—

_____   The impossible
is often the untried.

_____   —*Jim Goodwin*

_____

_____   _____

_____

_____

_____

_____

WHAT THE SCRIPTURES SAY

> Many, O LORD my God,
> are the wonders you have done.
> The things you planned for us
> no one can recount to you;
> were I to speak and tell of them,
> they would be too many to declare.
> —*Psalm 40:5*

Jesus looked at them and said, "With man this is impossible; all things are possible with God."

—*Mark 10:27*

A PRAYER FOR TODAY

God, I know You have removed my chains and paid the price for my forgiveness. You have freed me to overcome all obstacles, to leave the past behind and press forward into Your blessing. Forgive my unbelief, I pray, and teach me to walk forward in genuine, childlike faith.

_____

_____

_____

_____

Start by doing what's necessary,
then what's possible,
and suddenly you are doing
the impossible.

—*St. Francis of Assisi*

_____

_____

_____

_____

_____

TAKEAWAY TRUTH: God has given me free will. I can choose to change. Every right choice I make will overturn the wrong patterns that other people in my family's lineage have made.

DAY 6

A LASTING LEGACY

KEY TRUTH: Every time you honor God and do the right thing, you leave a lasting legacy that makes life easier for the generations that follow you.

My grandmother on my father's side worked extremely hard most of her life. My grandparents were cotton farmers and they lost everything they had in the Great Depression. My grandmother worked twelve hours a day earning ten cents an hour washing people's clothes: a dollar-twenty a day.

Grandmother never complained. She didn't go around with a "poor me" mentality; she just kept doing her best, giving it her all. She was determined and persistent. She may not have realized it, but she was sowing seeds for her children. She passed down hard work, determination, and persistence, which my father built upon. Because Grandmother laid the foundation, Daddy was able to break out of poverty and depression and raise our family to a completely new level.

My grandmother never really enjoyed the blessings and the favor that her descendants did. Had she not been willing to pay the price, my father may never have escaped poverty, and I might not be enjoying the season of usefulness that I am experiencing today.

CONSIDER THIS: When you get up early, work hard, and have a spirit of excellence, you are making a difference in your family's future. Don't be shortsighted and so ingrown that if it doesn't happen right now, you're not going to be happy. No, you are sowing the seeds that will reap a great harvest for generations to come. In the bloodline being formed in your DNA are your fortitude, strength, and excellent spirit. Reflect on the character and future you want for your children and grandchildren and the generations after them. In the space below, describe the ten qualities you value most for them, then reflect on the ways you are sowing the seeds of these qualities through your own life now.

_____

_____

_____

_____

_____

Nobody can do for little children
what grandparents do.
Grandparents sort of sprinkle
stardust over the lives
of little children.

—*Alex Haley*

_____

_____

_____

_____

_____

_____

_____

_____

> Lucky parents
> who have fine children
> usually have lucky children
> who have fine parents.
>
> —*James A. Brewer*

_____

_____

_____

_____

WHAT THE SCRIPTURES SAY

The righteous man leads a blameless life;
blessed are his children after him.
—*Proverbs 20:7*

Whatever you do, work at it with all your heart, as working for the Lord, not for men, since you know that you will receive an inheritance from the Lord as a reward.
—*Colossians 3:23–24*

A PRAYER FOR TODAY

Lord, I thank You for the family You gave me and the ones who went before me, breaking free of hardship and working with strong hearts so that my life could be better. You have given me the talents and gifts to make a better life for those who come after me. I pray that You'll give me the grace and faith to live up to this high calling. Let it be a strong testimony to Your love and faithfulness.

_____

_____

_____

_____

_____

_____

_____

_____

_____

_____

_____

_____

_____

_____

_____

TAKEAWAY TRUTH: I will get up every day and give it my best effort. God has promised that my family lines for up to a thousand generations are going to have the blessings and the favor of God because of the life that I've lived.

DAY 7

DIVINE DESTINY

KEY TRUTH: When you follow the destiny God has given you, you will live with passion and enthusiasm.

From the time I was ten or eleven years old, I was fascinated with television production. I loved the cameras, editing, and the production of television shows and movies. Every part of the process excited me. As a young man, I spent most of my weekends at Lakewood Church, where my father was the senior pastor. At the time, the church owned some small industrial cameras, and I'd spend all day Saturday playing with the equipment. I didn't really know how to run it, but I was fascinated by it. I'd turn the camera on and off, unplug it, plug it back in, coil the cables, and get the equipment ready for Sunday. I was passionate about it because it was what came naturally to me.

When I got old enough—maybe thirteen or fourteen years of age—I began helping to run the camera during the services; I became pretty good at it, too. In fact, I soon became one of the best cameramen that we had. It wasn't hard for me; quite the contrary, I loved it. To me, working behind the camera seemed almost like a hobby.

Looking back, I see now that my love for television production was part of my God-given destiny. God had hardwired that into me before the foundation of the world.

I went to college and studied broadcasting for a year, returned home, and started a full-fledged television ministry at Lakewood Church. Today I am on the other side of the cameras, and I can see how God was guiding my steps and preparing me for the fulfillment of my destiny.

CONSIDER THIS: You may not like the field in which you are working. You may dread going to your job. The work may feel meaningless and mundane. If so, reexamine what you are doing. You are not meant to live a miserable and unfulfilled life. Make sure that you are in a field that is part of your destiny. When you discover your destiny, and start working in some realm associated with it, you will thrive. Take some time right now to think about what compels you, what you feel passionate about. Name it in the space below, then describe what you've done with it so far. List three steps you could take to make your passion central in your life.

Since God made us
to be originals, why stoop
to be a copy?

—*Rev. Billy Graham*

_____

_____

_____

_____

_____   I'd rather be a failure
at something I enjoy than
_____   be a success at something
I hate.
_____
—*George Burns*
_____

_____   _____

_____

_____

_____

_____

WHAT THE SCRIPTURES SAY

For you created my inmost being;
you knit me together in my mother's womb.
I praise you because I am fearfully and wonderfully made;
your works are wonderful,
I know that full well.

—*Psalm 139:13–14*

In him we were also chosen, having been predestined according to the plan of him who works out everything in conformity with the purpose of his will, in order that we, who were the first to hope in Christ, might be for the praise of his glory.

—*Ephesians 1:11–12*

A PRAYER FOR TODAY

Lord, You made me and gifted me with desires, dreams, and passions. I praise You for the wonderful ways in which You prepared me before the foundations of the earth for my calling. Please guide me into the highest fulfillment of Your plans for me. Let my choices reflect Your plans and show the world Your glory and lovingkindness.

_____

_____

_____

_____

_____

_____

_____

_____

_____

_____

_____

_____

_____

TAKEAWAY TRUTH: I will make the decision to keep pressing forward, keep believing, and keep stretching until I see my dreams fulfilled. I know that one day, I will look back and say with confidence, "This is why God put me here."

STEP TWO

Be Positive Toward Yourself

DAY 1

A GOOD LISTENER

KEY TRUTH: To become a better you, you have to stop listening to the wrong voices.

Sometimes when I walk off the platform, having spoken at Lakewood and around the world by means of television, the first thought that comes to my mind is, *Joel, that message just wasn't good today. Nobody got anything out of that. You practically put them to sleep.*

I've learned to shake that off. I turn it around and say, "No, I believe it was good! I did my best. I know that at least one person really got something out of it: I did."

The Apostle Paul once said, "The things I know I should do, I don't. The things I know I shouldn't do, I end up doing." Even this great man of God who wrote half the New Testament struggled in this regard. That tells me God does not disqualify me merely because I don't perform perfectly 100 percent of the time. I wish I did, and I'm constantly striving to do better. I don't do wrong on purpose, but like anyone else, I too have weaknesses. Sometimes I make mistakes or wrong choices, but I have learned not to beat myself up over those things. I don't wallow in condemnation; I refuse to listen to the accusing voice. I know God is still working on me, that I'm growing, learning, and becoming a better me. I have made up my mind that I'm not going to live con-demned during the process.

CONSIDER THIS: As long as you have asked God to forgive you, and you are pressing forward in the direction He wants you to go, you can know with confidence God is pleased with you. In the spaces below, identify the ways in which you are tempted to believe accusing voices. Is it in a relationship, in the work you do, in certain habits that you'd like to break? Write it down. After each "accusation," write this: "God has made me worthy. I know God has great things in store for me."

_____

_____

_____

_____

＊＊＊

In order that all men may be
taught to speak truth,
it is necessary that all likewise
should learn to hear it.

—*Samuel Johnson*

_____

_____

_____

_____   ❧

_____   Most of the shadows
                                           of this life are caused
_____   by our standing in our own
                                                 sunshine.
_____
                                          —*Ralph Waldo Emerson*
_____

_____

_____

_____

_____

WHAT THE SCRIPTURES SAY

The LORD will fulfill his purpose for me;
your love, O LORD, endures forever—
do not abandon the works of your hands.
    —*Psalm 138:8*

Finally, be strong in the Lord and in his mighty power. Put on the
full armor of God so that you can take your stand against the
devil's schemes. . . . Stand firm then, with the belt of truth buckled
around your waist, with the breastplate of righteousness in place.
    —*Ephesians 6:10–11, 14*

A PRAYER FOR TODAY

God, I've made mistakes, but I know You love me, and I'm asking for forgiveness; I'm receiving Your mercy. Please give me the grace to go out each day expecting Your blessings and favor. Teach me to forget my failures in the way that You have.

_____

_____

_____

_____

_____

_____

_____

_____

_____

_____

_____

_____

_____

_____

_____

TAKEAWAY TRUTH: I have received God's mercy. I may not be perfect, but I'm growing. I may have made mistakes, but I'm forgiven. This is a new day. I'm not looking back—I'm looking forward.

DAY 2

JUST AS YOU ARE

KEY TRUTH: When you ask for God's forgiveness, you receive His mercy. You can expect God's blessings and favor.

Sam asks God to forgive him every day for something he did three years ago. He has asked for forgiveness more than five hundred times for the same thing. Sam fails to grasp the fact that God forgave him the first time he asked. The problem is, Sam didn't receive the forgiveness and mercy. He continues listening to the accusing voices: "You blew it. God can't bless you. You know what you did a few years ago."

As a parent, I don't focus on what our children do wrong. Our child can strike out a thousand times at the Little League field, but we'll go around bragging about the one hit he got all year long. Our son Jonathan is not perfect. He makes mistakes, and it is my joy to teach him, to train him, to help him come up higher. That's the way God is with us. He loves us unconditionally.

If you take hold of this truth, it will break the bonds that have held you back for years. Quit going around feeling wrong about yourself. If you're living your life condemned, that's telling me you're not receiving God's mercy. At times you may think, *I don't feel like I deserve it. I don't feel like I'm worthy.*

But that's what grace is all about. None of us deserves it. It's a free gift. We're not worthy in ourselves. The good news is, God has made us worthy.

CONSIDER THIS: God does not focus on what's wrong with you. He focuses on what's right with you. He's not looking at all your faults and weaknesses. He's looking at how far you've come, and how much you're growing. Look at yourself right now as though you were your own loving parent—the way God looks at you. Reject all your self-condemning thoughts, and write a description of all your qualities on which a loving parent would focus.

_____

_____

_____

The day the child realizes
that all adults are imperfect
he becomes an adolescent;
the day he forgives them,
he becomes an adult;
the day he forgives himself
he becomes wise.

—*Alden Nowlan*

_____

_____

_____

_____

_____

_____

_____

_____

_____

_____

_____

_____

_____

A forgiveness ought to be
like a canceled note, torn in two
and burned up, so that it can
never be shown against the man.

—*Henry Ward Beecher*

WHAT THE SCRIPTURES SAY

For it is by grace you have been saved, through faith—and this not
from yourselves, it is the gift of God—not by works, so that no
one can boast. For we are God's workmanship, created in Christ
Jesus to do good works, which God prepared in advance for us
to do.

—Ephesians 2:8–10

For we do not have a high priest who is unable to sympathize with
our weaknesses, but we have one who has been tempted in every
way, just as we are—yet was without sin. Let us then approach the
throne of grace with confidence, so that we may receive mercy and
find grace to help us in our time of need.

—Hebrews 4:15–16

A PRAYER FOR TODAY

Father, thank You that Your mercy endures forever. I may have made mistakes in the past, but I know nothing I've done is too much for Your mercy. I may have even made mistakes yesterday. But I know Your mercy is fresh and new this morning. So I receive it by faith today.

_____

_____

_____

_____

_____

_____

_____

_____

_____

_____

_____

_____

_____

TAKEAWAY TRUTH: I will reject negative thoughts toward myself and others. Instead, I will continually remind myself: God is pleased with me. God approves me. God accepts me just the way I am.

DAY 3

LETTING GO AND HOLDING ON

KEY TRUTH: Nothing you've done is too much for the mercy of God.

I love the story Jesus told about the prodigal son. This young man made a lot of mistakes. He told his dad that he wanted his share of the inheritance. When the father gave the son his money, the boy left home, went out and lived a wild life. Eventually, those poor choices caught up to him. When his money ran out, so did his friends. He didn't have anything to eat, any place to stay, and he ended up working in a hog pen feeding the pigs. He got so desperate and low, he had to eat the hog food just to stay alive.

One day, sitting in that filth and shame, he said to himself, "I will arise and go back to my father's house." That was the best decision that he ever made. The young man headed home, and I'm sure in the back of his mind he thought, *I'm just wasting my time. My father is never going to receive me back. I've made so many terrible choices.*

When the father saw his son coming from a distance, he took off running toward him. He couldn't wait to see him. When the father got there, he embraced his son, he was so happy to see him. But the son just hung his head in shame. He started to say, "I don't deserve any of this, but maybe you could take me back as one of your hired servants." The father answered, "What are you talking about? You are my son. I want to celebrate the fact that you are home."

CONSIDER THIS: When you make mistakes, when you go through failures and disappointments, don't sit around in self-pity. Don't go month after month condemning yourself, rejecting yourself. The first step to victory is to get back up again and go back to your Heavenly Father's loving arms. In the space below, reflect on how it feels to accept the good news that God's face will always be turned toward you. As you write, put aside all the shame you feel for past and present failures. Concentrate on the truth of God's acceptance.

_____

_____

_____

All the art of living lies
in the fine mingling of letting go
and holding on.

—*Havelock Ellis*

_____

_____

_____

_____

_____

_____

_____

_____

_____

_____

_____

_____

_____

WHAT THE SCRIPTURES SAY

Do you not know?
Have you not heard?
The LORD is the everlasting God,
the Creator of the ends of the earth. He will not grow tired or weary,
and his understanding no one can fathom.
He gives strength to the weary
and increases the power of the weak.
. . . those who hope in the LORD
will renew their strength.
They will soar on wings like eagles;
they will run and not grow weary,
they will walk and not be faint.

—*Isaiah 40:28–29, 31*

For it is with your heart that you believe and are justified, and it is
with your mouth that you confess you are saved. As the Scripture
says, "Anyone who trusts in him will never be put to shame."

—*Romans 10:10–11*

A PRAYER FOR TODAY

Lord, You are a loving, merciful, forgiving God. Thank You for being my Heavenly Father, setting me free of my mistakes and wrongs to live the bright future You have prepared for me. Give me the confidence, I pray, to receive Your acceptance and love as a trusting child.

Sorrow looks back,
worry looks around,
faith looks up.

—*Unknown*

TAKEAWAY TRUTH: I'm not going through life feeling guilty and unworthy. No mistake I've made is too horrible. I've repented. I've asked for forgiveness. Now, I'm going to take it one step further and start receiving God's mercy.

DAY 4

YOUR OWN BEST FRIEND

KEY TRUTH: You can be assured that God is pleased with you. God is not looking at what you've done wrong; He's looking at what you've done right.

I heard a story about a man and his small son who were hiking up a mountain. Suddenly, the little boy slipped and slid about thirty yards down the mountainside, getting caught in some brush. Unhurt but frightened, he called out, "Somebody, help me!"

A voice called back, "Somebody, help me!"

The youngster looked surprised and confused. He said, "Who are you?" The voice shouted back, "Who are you?"

The boy began to get aggravated. "You're a coward!" he yelled. The voice shouted back, "You're a coward!"

The boy shot back, "You're a fool." The voice repeated, "You're a fool."

By then the boy's father had reached him and helped extricate his son from the brush. The boy looked up and said, "Dad, who is that?" The father chuckled and said, "Son, that's called an echo, but it's also called life. Let me show you something." The dad shouted out, "You're a winner!" The voice shouted back, "You're a winner!" The dad's voice boomed, "You've got what it takes." The voice boomed back, "You've got what it takes."

"Son, that's exactly how it is in life," the father explained. "Whatever you send out always comes back to you."

CONSIDER THIS: What messages are you sending out about yourself? Are they negative messages? ("I'm a failure. I'm unattractive. I'm undisciplined. I'm broke. I've got a terrible temper.") Or do you remember that you are the apple of God's eye? Right now, in the space below, write the positive messages about yourself that you can start sending out ("I'm approved, I'm accepted, I am the righteousness of God. I am creative. I am talented. I am more than a conqueror.")

_____

_____

_____

_____

We are all worms,
but I do believe I am
a glowworm.

—*Winston Churchill*

_____

_____

_____

_____   ━━━━━━ ⟨⟩ ━━━━━━

_____

_____   We have to learn
                                             to be our own best friends,
_____   because we fall too easily
                                             into the trap of being
_____   our worst enemies.

_____   —*Roderick Thorp*

_____

_____

_____

_____

WHAT THE SCRIPTURES SAY

For the sake of his great name the LORD will not reject his people,
because the LORD was pleased to make you his own.

—*1 Samuel 12:22*

A generous man will prosper;
he who refreshes others will himself be refreshed.

—*Proverbs 11:25*

Remember this: Whoever sows sparingly will also reap sparingly,
and whoever sows generously will also reap generously.

—*2 Corinthians 9:6*

A PRAYER FOR TODAY

God, I know You approve me, so I feel good about myself. Please gift me with confidence in Your Fatherly love. I know I have these areas I need to improve, but I'm doing my best. I'm making up my mind that I am going to go through this day feeling good about me, because You have already accepted and approved me.

TAKEAWAY TRUTH: I will get up every morning and even though I make mistakes, I will boldly say, "God, I know You approve me, so I feel good about who I am."

DAY 5

WORDS OF LOVE

KEY TRUTH: You have the seeds of greatness inside of you, but it is up to you to believe and act on them. Your words will set the direction of your life.

Many people suffer a poor self-image because of their own words. They've gone around for years putting themselves down, and now they've developed wrong mind-sets that prevent them from rising higher in their careers or in their personal lives.

"Joel, I've made so many mistakes I don't see how God could bless me," Catherine said through her tears. "I just don't feel like I deserve it."

"No, we don't deserve God's blessings," I told her. "They are part of the free gift of God's salvation. The best thing you could do is to accept His offer, and all through the day start saying to yourself, 'I am a new creation. I am forgiven. I am valuable to God. He has made me worthy.' If you keep saying that long enough, you're going to start believing it. And you will begin expecting good things."

Positively or negatively, creative power resides in your words, because you believe your own words more than you believe anybody else's. Think about it. Your words go out of your mouth and they come right back into your own ears. If you hear those comments long enough, they will drop down into your spirit and produce exactly what you're saying. That's why it is so important that we get in a habit of declaring good things over our lives every day.

CONSIDER THIS: God didn't create any of us to be average. He didn't make us to barely get by. We were created to excel. The Scripture teaches that before the foundation of the world, God not only chose us, but He equipped us with everything we need to live His abundant life. In the space below, list some of the negative words you repeat about yourself to yourself. Then take each one and rewrite it so that it is transformed into a positive statement.

_____

_____

_____

_____

Learn a new language
and get a new soul.

—*Czech proverb*

_____

_____

_____

_____

_____

_____   ⚬

_____

_____   To speak of "mere words"
                            is much like speaking of
_____   "mere dynamite."

_____   —*C. J. Ducasse*

_____

_____   _____

_____

_____

_____

_____

WHAT THE SCRIPTURES SAY

Let the beloved of the Lord rest secure in him,
for He shields him all day long,
and the one the LORD loves rests between his shoulders.

> —*Deuteronomy 33:12*

But you are a chosen people, a royal priesthood, a holy nation, a
people belonging to God.

> —*1 Peter 2:9*

Do your best to present yourself to God as one approved, a work-
man who does not need to be ashamed and who correctly handles
the word of truth.

> —*2 Timothy 2:15*

A PRAYER FOR TODAY

God, thank You for being pleased with me, for accepting and approving me. Forgive me for the wrong choices I make and teach me to remember that I have entrusted my life to You. Help me to make healthy, positive choices that will bring honor to Your name and wholeness to my life.

_____

_____

_____

_____

_____

_____

_____

_____

_____

_____

_____

_____

_____

_____

_____

TAKEAWAY TRUTH: Today will be a turning point in my life. Starting today, I will make positive declarations over my own life. I will say things like, "I am blessed. I am healthy and prosperous. I am competent. I am called. I'm anointed. I'm creative. I'm talented. I am well able to fulfill my destiny."

DAY 6

THOUGHTS OF AFFIRMATION

KEY TRUTH: You can have confidence in yourself because you are a child of the Most High God. You have been crowned with God's glory and honor. You can do all things through Christ.

When Moses was born, the Egyptian Pharaoh decreed that all the Jewish children two years of age and under would be killed. Instead of acquiescing to the absurd, diabolical command, Moses's mother hid him away. Eventually she put him in a basket and sent him down the Nile River. One of Pharaoh's daughters found him and raised him. Because Moses didn't grow up around a godly father, he didn't have that person speaking blessings into his life.

Many years later, God came to Moses and said, "Moses, I'm choosing you to deliver the people of Israel." Not surprisingly, the first words out of Moses's mouth were, "God, who am I?" Then Moses asked another question. He said, "God, who will listen to me? You know I'm not a good speaker. You know I stutter." Notice his lack of confidence. He was playing the wrong recording in his mind. Possibly his confidence had been undermined by having an absentee father, by missing a parent who spoke good things into his life on a regular basis. With God's help, however, Moses overcame that deficit in his upbringing.

You must get your thoughts about yourself moving in the

right direction if you truly want to become a better you. All through the day, you should be thinking good things about you.

CONSIDER THIS: You are full of potential. You are overflowing with creativity. There's nothing in your heart that you cannot accomplish. You have courage, strength, and ability. The favor of God surrounds you wherever you go. That's who you really are. So you can throw back your shoulders, hold your head up high, and speak positive affirmations and faith-filled words over your life. In the space below, write ten statements that affirm positive truths about who you are.

_____

_____

_____

_____

When you say a situation   _____
or a person is hopeless,
you are slamming the door   _____
in the face of God.

—*Rev. Charles L. Allen*   _____

_____

_____

_____

_____

_____

_____

_____

_____

_____

_____

_____

_____

_____   The summit of happiness
                                                 is reached when a person
_____   is ready to be what he is.

_____   —*Erasmus*

_____

_____

_____

_____

_____

_____

WHAT THE SCRIPTURES SAY

I am still confident of this:
I will see the goodness of the LORD
in the land of the living.
                    —*Psalm 27:13*

As God's fellow workers we urge you not to receive God's grace in
vain. For he says, "In the time of my favor I heard you, and in the
day of salvation I helped you." I tell you, now is the time of
God's favor, now is the day of salvation.
                    —*2 Corinthians 6:1–2*

A PRAYER FOR TODAY

Father, You have loved me and blessed me. You have anointed me to do Your will. You have enabled me and made me victorious, endowed with Your greatness. I will praise Your Holy Name. Your mercy endures forever.

_____

_____

_____

_____

_____

_____

_____

_____

_____

_____

_____

_____

_____

_____

_____

TAKEAWAY TRUTH: As of today, I will have confidence in myself. I will choose to put on a positive recording and tell myself, "I am forgiven. I am restored. God has a new plan. He has good things in store for me."

DAY 7

THE NEW SELF

KEY TRUTH: Knowing and acknowledging that you are fulfilling God's purpose for you will not only boost your confidence sky-high, it will enable *you* to rise higher and see God's blessings and favor in a greater way.

The other day I talked to a young woman in the lobby of Lakewood Church. She was beautiful, and by all outward appearances she seemed to be happy and on top of the world. On the inside, however, she had a war going on. She didn't like herself. She thought she was unattractive. She thought she was overweight. She had a long list of things she felt were wrong with her.

As I talked with her, I discovered that her father had always put her down. He constantly told her what was wrong with her, what she couldn't do, what she was never going to be. The sad thing is, this young lady in her late twenties had gone through two marriages and was now about to end her third.

I told her, "You've got the wrong recording playing on your internal CD player. You're constantly telling yourself, 'I'm fat. I'm unattractive. I have nothing to offer. I'm unlovable.' As long as you're dwelling on those lies, there's going to be a war on the inside. You were not created to live that way. God created you to feel good about yourself. If you cannot get along with yourself, you'll never be able to get along with other people."

CONSIDER THIS: You need to get at peace with who you are. Dwell only on positive, empowering thoughts toward yourself. That's when your faith will be energized. Reflect on the positive thoughts you have been practicing toward yourself this week. Then record in the space below the blessings and possibilities from God that are becoming clearer to you.

_____

_____

_____

Men go abroad to wonder at the heights
of mountains, at the huge waves of the sea,
at the long courses of the rivers,
at the vast compass of the ocean,
at the circular motions of the stars;
and they pass by themselves
without wondering.

—*St. Augustine*

_____

_____

_____

_____

_____

_____

_____

_____

_____

_____

> Our prayers are answered
> not when we are given
> what we ask but when we are
> challenged to be what we can be.
>
> —*Morris Adler*

_____

_____

_____

_____

_____

WHAT THE SCRIPTURES SAY

May the God of hope fill you with all joy and peace as you trust in him, so that you may overflow with hope by the power of the Holy Spirit. I myself am convinced, my brothers, that you yourselves are full of goodness, complete in knowledge and competent to instruct one another.

—*Romans 15:13–14*

You were taught, with regard to your former way of life, to put off your old self, which is being corrupted by its deceitful desires; to be made new in the attitude of your minds; and to put on the new self, created to be like God in true righteousness and holiness.

—*Ephesians 4:22–24*

A PRAYER FOR TODAY

Lord, You called me to be Your beloved child, gifted and valuable and blessed. I pray that You will lift me higher and higher to see Your blessings and favor in a greater way. Let my affirmations be a testimony to Your greatness and goodness today. May my attitudes honor You and reflect Your goodness.

_____

_____

_____

_____

_____

_____

_____

_____

_____

_____

_____

_____

_____

_____

_____

_____

TAKEAWAY TRUTH: I have a bright future. I have the favor of God. I will make a habit of acknowledging what's right with me.

STEP THREE

Develop Better Relationships

DAY 1

GIVING BACK

KEY TRUTH: When you believe the best in people, you help to bring the best out of them.

When I was in middle school, I was one of the smaller players on the basketball team. In our first game of the season, we were scheduled to face a really good team, boasting a bunch of big guys. Naturally, at my size, it would have been easy to be intimidated by our opponents.

On game day, I was walking through the school hallways in between classes when my basketball coach called me over to where he was standing in front of several of my friends. He was a big, strong, rough coach, and in his usual gruff manner, he said, "Joel, you're not that tall, but let me tell you, size doesn't matter. What counts is right down in here." He pointed his finger at his chest as he continued. "Joel, you've got a big heart, and you're going to do great this year."

When I heard the coach's words—spoken right in front of my friends—I stood up taller, threw my shoulders back, and smiled even more than usual! You would have thought I was Michael Jordan. I thought to myself, *The coach believes in me!* My confidence shot up to a completely new level, and I played better that year than I'd ever done before. It's amazing what we can accomplish when we know somebody really believes in us.

That coach took a little time to make a big difference. He took time to instill confidence in me. If we're going to bring out the best in people, we too need to sow seeds of encouragement.

CONSIDER THIS: God puts people in our lives on purpose so we can help them succeed and help them become all He created them to be. Most people will not reach their full potential without somebody else believing in them. Think back and identify three people who encouraged you at some point, then describe how each one showed that they believed in you. After you've completed this, identify three people who you can encourage.

_____

_____

_____

The bitterest tears
shed over graves are
for words left unsaid
and deeds left undone.

—*Harriet Beecher Stowe*

_____

_____

_____

_____

_____

_____

_____

_____

The genius of communication
is the ability to be both totally
honest and totally kind
at the same time.

—John Powell

_____

_____

_____

_____

_____

_____

_____

WHAT THE SCRIPTURES SAY

Do not let any unwholesome talk come out of your mouths, but
only what is helpful for building others up according to their
needs, that it may benefit those who listen.

—Ephesians 4:29

Therefore, encourage one another and build each other up, just as
in fact you are doing.

—1 Thessalonians 5:11

A PRAYER FOR TODAY

Father, You are working in me to bring out my best. I pray that You will teach me to speak words of encouragement to others so they can hear Your voice through my words. You are a kind and loving Heavenly Father. Make me a child who is worthy of the love I've been given.

_____

_____

_____

_____

_____

_____

_____

_____

_____

_____

_____

_____

_____

_____

TAKEAWAY TRUTH: I will help somebody else become successful and trust God to make me successful. This week I will build up, encourage, or otherwise improve the lives of at least three people.

DAY 2

PEOPLE INVESTMENTS

KEY TRUTH: If you will make somebody else's day, God will make yours.

Brent, a man who attends Lakewood Church, was standing in line at the grocery store checkout waiting to pay for his selections. The young woman running the register was having a tough time. People in line started getting aggravated and being a bit short with her.

When it was Brent's turn to check out, he decided he wasn't going to add to the problem by responding the way others had done. He smiled and said, "Ma'am, I just want to tell you that I think you're doing a great job. I appreciate you working so hard."

That young woman's countenance brightened instantly. It was as though Brent had lifted a load of heavy bricks off her shoulders. "Sir, I've been working here for three months," she said, "and you are the first person to tell me anything like that. Thank you so much."

Our society overflows with critics, cynics, and faultfinders. Many people quickly point out what you are doing wrong, but relatively few take the time to point out anything you are doing right.

CONSIDER THIS: The Scripture says, "Iron sharpens iron." The way we live our lives with one another should encourage us to do better. Use the space below to reflect on these questions: "How are the people in my life better off because I passed their way? Am I building them up in our conversations, and bringing out their best, or am I dragging them down? How can I show my companions that I believe in them?"

_____

_____

_____

_____

Life is short
and we never have enough time
for gladdening the hearts
of those who travel the way
with us. Oh, be swift to love!
Make haste to be kind.

—*Henri Frederic Amiel*

_____

_____

_____

_____

⸻⸺✼⸺⸻

_____   Those who bring sunshine
to the lives of others
_____   cannot keep it
from themselves.
_____
—*James Matthew Barrie*
_____

_____

_____

_____

_____

_____

_____

_____

_____

WHAT THE SCRIPTURES SAY

Let us therefore make every effort to do what leads to peace and mutual edification.

—*Romans 14:19*

We know that we all possess knowledge. Knowledge puffs up, *but love builds up.*

—*1 Corinthians 8:1*

A PRAYER FOR TODAY

Lord, You have blessed me with people in my life who believe in me. I pray that you'll make me a blessing in the lives of others. Help me to be a people builder, focused on bringing out the best in others. Show me the people, day by day, who need my expressions of affirmation and confidence in them.

_____

_____

_____

_____

_____

_____

_____

_____

_____

_____

_____

_____

_____

_____

_____

TAKEAWAY TRUTH: I will choose to bring out the best in the people whom God has put in my life. The investment I make in other people's lives will last forever.

DAY 3

A BLANKET OF LOVE

KEY TRUTH: To keep the strife out of our lives, we must learn how to give people the benefit of the doubt.

Christine was driving through an intersection when she accidentally turned too sharply and sideswiped another car. Worse yet, she was driving her brand-new car, a wedding gift from her husband Eric. Christine pulled over to the side of the road and the driver of the other car, an older gentleman, got out of his car and began to examine his severely damaged front bumper. He then stepped over to where Christine was sitting in her car, crying.

"Are you okay, young lady?" he asked kindly.

"I'm fine," Christine sobbed, "but I just got married and my husband gave me this car as a wedding gift; he is going to be so upset. I don't know what I'm going to do."

"Oh, I'm sure it will be okay," the older gentleman tried to console her. "Your husband will understand." They talked for a few minutes before he said, "If I could just get your insurance information, we'll exchange that, and be on our way."

"I don't even know if I have an insurance card," Christine said through her tears.

"Well, it is usually in the glove compartment," the man suggested. "Why don't you check there?"

Christine opened the glove compartment and found the owner's registration and the insurance information. Attached to the envelope containing the insurance card was a note that read, "Honey, just in case you ever have an accident, please remember I love you and not the car."

CONSIDER THIS: If we expect people to be perfect, it is not fair to them, and it will be a source of frustration for us. We will always be disappointed. Your frustrations with people close to you reveal your unrealistic expectations about those people. In the space below, reflect on ways in which you are expecting perfection and how specifically you can change your attitude to one that builds up the people you love.

_____

_____

_____

_____

Kindness consists
in loving people
more than they deserve.

—*Joseph Joubert*

_____

_____

_____

_____

_____

_____   ———————⚮———————

_____   Kind words can be short
                                          and easy to speak, but their
_____   echoes are truly endless.

_____   —*Mother Teresa of Calcutta*

_____   ————————————————

_____

_____

_____

_____

_____

WHAT THE SCRIPTURES SAY

Bear with each other and forgive whatever grievances you may
have against one another. Forgive as the Lord forgave you.

—*Colossians 3:13*

Above all, love each other deeply, because love covers over a mul-
titude of sins.

—*1 Peter 4:8*

A PRAYER FOR TODAY

Father, how thankful I am that I am forgiven, and that You have held none of my mistakes and wrongdoing against me. I want to love others as You have loved me and to forgive others as You have forgiven me. Please grant me the grace and goodness to keep no record of wrongs done to me. Give me Your vision to look for and find the good You have placed in others around me.

_____

_____

_____

_____

_____

_____

_____

_____

_____

_____

_____

_____

_____

TAKEAWAY TRUTH: I will be the kind of person who shows mercy, even in advance of someone else's mistake or wrong action. Rather than flaunting somebody's failure, I'll learn to cover his/her weakness with forgiveness.

DAY 4

BLESSED ARE THE PEACEMAKERS

KEY TRUTH: When you sow seeds of mercy and kindness, you'll begin to see your relationships improve.

I recently spoke with a man who was broken and defeated. When I asked him what was troubling him, he explained how he and his father got at odds with each other over a business decision. They hadn't spoken in more than two years. He said, "Joel, I knew deep down inside that I needed to make it right, but I kept putting it off. Then earlier this week, I received a call informing me that my father had suffered a heart attack and died." Imagine what emotional pain that man is living with.

Don't wait until you cannot make amends with someone from whom you are estranged. Do it today; swallow your pride and apologize even if it wasn't your fault. Keep the peace. Understand, it's not always about being right. It's about keeping strife out of your life. You can win every argument, but if it opens the door to turmoil, brings division, and tears you apart, in the end you didn't win at all—and you may have lost a lot. If you wait for somebody else to be the peacemaker in your life, you may wait around your whole lifetime, living your life on hold.

CONSIDER THIS: God always gives us a warning, a wake-up call of sorts. He may say simply, "Stop being so argumentative. Quit being a faultfinder. Quit keeping your record books. Start being a peacemaker." When we recognize His voice, we need to respond. Search your heart right now, and listen for God's urging. What's listed in *your* record book against another person? Acknowledge it in the space below. Then write out a plan for how you will make things right with that person. Be specific and set a time limit for doing it.

_____

_____

_____

_____

One of the most lasting pleasures
you can experience is the feeling
that comes over you when you
genuinely forgive an enemy—
whether he knows it or not.

—O. A. Battista

_____

_____

_____

_____   ❧

_____   Forgiving and being forgiven
                                       are two names for
_____   the same thing. The important
                                       thing is that a discord
_____   has been resolved.

_____   —C. S. Lewis

_____   _____

_____

_____

_____

_____

_____

WHAT THE SCRIPTURES SAY

> Blessed are the peacemakers,
> for they shall be called sons of God.
> —*Matthew 5:9*

But the wisdom that comes from heaven is first of all pure; then peace-loving, considerate, submissive, full of mercy and good fruit, impartial and sincere. Peacemakers who sow in peace raise a harvest of righteousness.

—*James 3:17–18*

A PRAYER FOR TODAY

Father, only You can change people. Only You can make a new work of a human being. Please help me to honor You by leaving the changing up to You and concentrating on forgiving others. Teach me how to do my part to keep strife out of my relationships.

_____

_____

_____

_____

_____

_____

_____

_____

_____

_____

_____

_____

_____

_____

_____

_____

_____

_____

_____

TAKEAWAY TRUTH: Peace starts with me. I will commit myself to making the first move, wherever I have been at odds with another person.

DAY 5

FAMILY TIES THAT BIND

KEY TRUTH: If we're going to have strong, healthy relationships, we must dig our heels in and fight for our families. If we will do our part and take a strong stand for our families, God will do His part to help us have great relationships with our parents and children.

Mandy grew up in a dysfunctional home. Her father was never around and her mother had plenty of problems of her own. As a teenager, Mandy raised her younger brother. To all observers, it appeared that Mandy was handling the situation reasonably well, but on the inside, she was crying out for help.

One day a friend of hers at school mentioned that her father owned a fast-food restaurant. "Come on down, Mandy. Maybe my dad will give you a job," her friend suggested. Mandy visited the restaurant, and that gentleman not only gave her a job, but he also took her under his wing. He began to watch after her, making sure she changed the oil in her car, checking to see that she was doing okay in school, and on and on. He didn't even realize it, but he became the father figure for which Mandy longed. Years later, when Mandy was about to get married, her real father was nowhere to be found. Can you guess who gave Mandy away at her wedding?

That's right; it was the man from the fast-food restaurant. He made time to care. He fought not only for his own family; he fought for somebody else's child, too. Today, Mandy is healthy, whole, and happily married, much to the credit of a man who became a father figure to her.

CONSIDER THIS: One of the greatest threats we face in the twenty-first century is not a terrorist attack or an ecological catastrophe, but an attack on our homes. Too many homes are being destroyed through strife, lack of commitment, wrong priorities, and bad attitudes. But God holds us responsible for keeping our families together. If we'll do our part, God will do His. Listen carefully to yourself as you relate to your family in the coming week. Do you complain and emphasize what family members are not doing right? Or do you bless, encourage, uplift, and compliment them? Describe your typical response below and consider how you would like to shape it in the future.

_____

_____

Children are like wet cement. Whatever falls on them makes an impression.

—*Haim Ginott*

_____

_____

_____

_____

_____

Seldom do parents have trouble
with children when the Bible
is read regularly in the home.

—*Rev. Billy Graham*

_____

_____

_____

WHAT THE SCRIPTURES SAY

These commandments that I give you today are to be upon your hearts. Impress them on your children. Talk about them when you sit at home and when you walk along the road, when you lie down and when you get up.

Deuteronomy 6:6–7

Train a child in the way he should go,
and when he is old he will not turn from it.
—*Proverbs 22:6*

Fathers, do not exasperate your children; instead, bring them up in the training and instruction of the Lord.

—*Ephesians 6:4*

A PRAYER FOR TODAY

Father, thank You for the family You have given me. I pray that You will equip me to love each family member with Your love, to encourage and build them up. Help me to put first things first, always saving my best time for these people who count on me. When someone comes along who needs a "family," let me be part of their healing; let me be family to them as You are family to each of us.

_____

_____

_____

_____

_____

What a father
says to his children
is not heard by the world;
but it will be heard
by posterity.

—*Jean Paul Richter*

_____

_____

_____

_____

_____

_____

_____

_____

TAKEAWAY TRUTH: I will do my best to create an atmosphere of peace and unity in my home. I will reach out to children who don't have a father figure or a mother figure and help them discover their identity.

DAY 6

BETTER TO GIVE

KEY TRUTH: If you want your relationships to thrive, you must invest in them by being a giver rather than taker.

Years ago when Colin Powell worked for President Ronald Reagan, he and several other Cabinet members came up with a new policy. They were excited about it and went to a meeting with President Reagan to explain the details.

General Powell felt strongly about it because it was his idea, so he was selling the program to the best of his ability. He told President Reagan how helpful the new system could be, but President Reagan wasn't convinced. He saw what he thought were some major flaws. After some debate, even though he disagreed, President Reagan decided to trust General Powell and accepted the new policy.

Unfortunately, the policy totally failed and created a huge mess. At a press conference, President Reagan was questioned about what went wrong. After an intense grilling of the president, a reporter finally asked the question General Powell hoped would not be asked: "Mr. President, tell us, was this new policy your idea?"

Without hesitation President Reagan said, "I take full responsibility for it." General Powell stood on the side of the room, and he had tears in his eyes. The president had just made a huge investment in his relationship with General Powell by protecting his reputation and covering his mistake. General Powell told one of the other Cabinet members, "I'll do anything for that man."

CONSIDER THIS: Your words have the power to put a spring in somebody's step, to lift somebody out of defeat and discouragement, and to help propel them to victory. Everyone you know needs that sort of encouragement. Think of ten investments you can make this week in the lives of people you love and record them in the space below.

_____

_____

_____

_____

<hr/>

If you want your children
to improve, let them overhear
the nice things you say
about them to others.

—*Haim Ginott*

_____

_____

_____

_____

_____

_____

_____

_____

_____

_____

_____

_____

_____

_____

_____

_____

_____   ⸎

_____

_____   Once in a century a man
                                          may be ruined or made
_____   insufferable by praise.
                                          But surely once in a minute
_____   something generous dies
                                          for want of it.
_____
                                          —*John Masefield*
_____

_____

_____

_____

_____

WHAT THE SCRIPTURES SAY

But encourage one another daily, as long as it is called Today, so
that none of you may be hardened by sin's deceitfulness.

—*Hebrews 3:13*

And let us consider how we may spur one another on toward love
and good deeds. Let us not give up meeting together, as some are
in the habit of doing, but let us encourage one another.

—*Hebrews 10:24–25*

A PRAYER FOR TODAY

Lord, You have blessed me with all sorts of blessings. I pray that You'll open my eyes to ways that I can bless others as I have been blessed. Please give me the grace to be a giver instead of a taker.

_____

_____

_____

_____

_____

_____

_____

_____

_____

_____

_____

_____

_____

_____

_____

_____

TAKEAWAY TRUTH: I will make sure I'm making relational investments wherever I go. Rather than being a taker who constantly makes withdrawals from the emotional reserves of other people, I will attempt to encourage everyone I meet.

DAY 7

GOD'S DELEGATE

KEY TRUTH: When you show love, you are showing God to the world.

I heard a story about a young boy who lived in the inner city. He was about eight years old, and his family was extremely poor. One cold fall day, he was up at the local store looking in the window admiring a pair of tennis shoes. As he stood there, cold and barefoot, a lady came along and said, "Young man, what are you doing staring so intently in this window?"

Under his breath, and almost shyly, he said, "Well, I was just sort of praying and asking God if He'd give me a new pair of tennis shoes."

Without hesitation, the woman took him into the store and very gently and lovingly washed his cold dirty feet. Then she put a brand-new pair of socks on him and told him to pick out three new pairs of tennis shoes. He couldn't believe it. He was so excited. He had never owned a new pair of shoes. He'd always worn hand-me-downs.

After the woman paid for the purchases, she returned to the little boy. He looked at her in disbelief. Nobody had ever taken that kind of interest in him. With tears running down his cheeks, he said, "Lady, can I ask you a question? Are you God's wife?"

CONSIDER THIS: You are never more like God than when you give, when you take time for people, when you do something good for somebody who can never repay you. Who do you know that you can be good to today? How can you be a blessing to someone who cannot repay you? Think of three people or ways that you can bless someone this week. Write them down below and be specific about what you plan to do.

_____

_____

_____

_____

_____

Great opportunities to help
others seldom come, but small
ones surround us every day.

—*Sally Koch*

_____

_____

_____

_____   ⟿

_____

_____   It is well to give when asked,
                                         but it is better to give unasked,
_____   through understanding.

_____   —*Kahlil Gibran*

_____   _____

_____

_____

_____

_____

_____

_____

WHAT THE SCRIPTURES SAY

He who receives you receives me, and he who receives me receives
the one who sent me. . . . And if anyone gives even a cup of cold
water to one of these little ones because he is my disciple, I tell you
the truth, he will certainly not lose his reward.

—*Matthew 10:40, 42*

Do not forget to entertain strangers, for by so doing some people
have entertained angels without knowing it.

—*Hebrews 13:2*

A PRAYER FOR TODAY

God, You have led the way in being the Giver of good gifts. You have loved me and blessed me and given me eternal life. I pray that You will make clear to me the many opportunities I have to follow Your example, to love others with the love You've offered me, and to give generously to all. Let my love be so full of action that others can see Your love in me.

_____

_____

_____

_____

_____

_____

_____

_____

_____

_____

_____

_____

_____

_____

_____

TAKEAWAY TRUTH: I really want to be a better me. I will start being good to people. I will pay attention to those around me and remember that true love is always backed up with actions.

STEP FOUR

Form Better Habits

DAY 1

FEEDING THE GOOD WOLF

KEY TRUTH: Successful people develop better habits. You can't keep doing the same things you have been doing and expect to get different results.

An old Cherokee tale tells of a grandfather teaching life principles to his grandson. The wise old Cherokee said, "Son, on the inside of every person a battle is raging between two wolves. One wolf is evil. It's angry, jealous, unforgiving, proud, and lazy. The other wolf is good. It's filled with love, kindness, humility, and self-control.

"These two wolves are constantly fighting," the grandfather said.

The little boy thought about it, and said, "Grandfather, which wolf is going to win?"

The grandfather smiled and said, "Whichever one you feed."

Feeding unforgiveness, impatience, low self-esteem, or other negative traits will only make them stronger. For instance, maybe you complain frequently about your job. You're always talking negatively about your boss, how that company doesn't treat you right, and how you can't stand the drive to work. Ironically, when we complain, we feel a sense of release. It feels good to feed those negative thoughts. But the wolf we feed will always want more.

The next time you are tempted to complain, ask yourself, "Do I really want to keep feeding this negative habit?" "Do I really want to stay where I am?" Or, "Do I want to starve this complaining spirit and step up higher?"

CONSIDER THIS: Your habits—whether good or bad—will greatly determine your future. One study says that 90 percent of our everyday behavior is based on our habits. That means how we treat people, how we spend our money, what we watch, what we listen to—90 percent of the time, we're on autopilot. We do what we've always done.

To become a better you, take inventory of your habits. Do you have a tendency to be negative in your thoughts and conversations? Are you always late to work? Do you worry all the time? Do you overeat? Do you regularly succumb to addictions? Use the space below to describe your daily life and identify any habits that are affecting your life negatively. Be specific and honest. You can't change what you won't acknowledge. When you're finished, choose at least one negative habit and describe a positive habit that can take its place.

_____

_____

_____

_____

_____

_____

_____

_____

_____

_____

_____

_____

_____

⁓

_____

You will stay young
as long as you learn,
form new habits,
and don't mind being
contradicted.

— *Marie von Ebner-Eschenbach*

_____

_____

_____

_____

WHAT THE SCRIPTURES SAY

Show me your ways, O LORD,
teach me your paths.
—*Psalm 25:4*

"Everything is permissible for me"—but not everything is beneficial. "Everything is permissible for me"—but I will not be mastered by anything.
—*1 Corinthians 6:12*

A PRAYER FOR TODAY

Lord, I want to make Your ways my ways. I have the desire, but I need the strength that comes from You to endure the discomfort change causes. Please help me see the habits in my life that do not honor You, and give me the power to overcome them.

_____

_____

_____

_____

_____

───────────❧───────────

Moral excellence comes about
as a result of habit. We become
just by doing just acts,
temperate by doing temperate acts,
brave by doing brave acts.

—*Aristotle*

TAKEAWAY TRUTH: I will examine my daily routine and begin to identify the negative habits that have become my "autopilot." I will commit myself to changing those habits to better ones.

DAY 2

WHATEVER IS NOBLE

KEY TRUTH: It's not so much that we *break* bad habits; we must *replace* them, and God already has a path of success laid out for you.

A young couple at Lakewood had about $40,000 in credit card debt. They were embarrassed and distraught over it. They didn't see any way out.

Then one day they took a step of faith; they swallowed their pride and met with one of our financial counselors at the ministry. That counselor studied their finances and gave them instructions in how they could overcome their financial problems, step by step.

The couple committed themselves to getting out of debt, and for three years they didn't go out to eat, they didn't take vacations, they didn't buy extra clothes. It was a bare-bones budget that was uncomfortable and a sacrifice.

They were overturning years of wrong choices, forming better habits, and establishing a foundation for years of right choices. They quit using their credit cards. They learned the difference between their wants and their needs. They started practicing discipline and self-control. Three years later, that young couple is totally debt-free and God is blessing them. They're seeing increase and promotion. And it all started when they decided to form better habits.

CONSIDER THIS: The first step to overcoming any habit or addiction is to identify what's holding you back. But don't stop there. Make a decision to do something about it. Take action. Don't be too embarrassed to seek help. You can change. Freedom is available. Think some more about the habits in your life that have a negative impact on you and others. In the space below, identify the places in which you need to reach out to others for help. Then do the research to find out to whom you can turn for counseling and encouragement. Make a plan right now to see them.

_____

_____

_____

———❦———

Let him who
would move the world,
first move himself.

—*Socrates*

_____

_____

_____

_____

_____

_____

_____

_____

_____

> Action may not always
> be happiness, but there is no
> happiness without action.
>
> —*Benjamin Disraeli*

_____

_____

_____

_____

_____

_____

_____

_____

WHAT THE SCRIPTURES SAY

No temptation has seized you except what is common to man. And God is faithful; he will not let you be tempted beyond what you can bear. But when you are tempted, he will also provide a way out so that you can stand up under it.

—*1 Corinthians 10:13*

Whatever is noble, whatever is right, whatever is pure, whatever is lovely, whatever is admirable—if anything is excellent or praiseworthy—think about such things.

—*Philippians 4:8*

A PRAYER FOR TODAY

God, I know I can't replace my bad habits under my own power. But I'm claiming the power of Your saving love in my life to make the changes I need to make. I pray that You will walk before me and make my path straight so I am mastered by nothing. Please bring the helpers into my life that I need to work through any addictions or dependencies that have had an impact on my life.

_____

_____

_____

_____

_____

_____

_____

_____

_____

_____

_____

_____

_____

_____

_____

TAKEAWAY TRUTH: I will get my negative habits under control. I will seek the help of God and His helpers whenever I need it. And I'll be free.

DAY 3

LIVING JOY

KEY TRUTH: Happiness is a choice that you make. It does not depend on your circumstances.

One time, Victoria and I had the perfect vacation planned. We had been looking forward to it for several months. It was an opportunity for just the two of us to get away together and take a break for a few days. The closer I got to the vacation dates, the more excited I became. I had my tickets and I was ready to go.

My mother had been dealing with a hip problem due to a bout with polio she had suffered when she was a child. When the doctors had done their best to treat my mother with medicine, they decided that they were going to have to replace her hip, so they scheduled her for surgery. Something came up right at the last minute, and they had to reschedule that surgery. The postponed surgery date fell on the exact same day Victoria and I planned to leave for our big trip. I had a tough decision to make: whether I was going to go on vacation or stay home and take care of my mother. We decided to stay home. At first we were disappointed, but we decided we weren't going to let that steal our joy.

Mother had the surgery, and that week while I was at the hospital visiting her, I must have prayed for twenty or thirty other people, too. At one point, I was going from hospital room to hospital room, as one family after another asked me to pray for their loved one. At the end of that week, I felt more refreshed and more relaxed than I would have had I gone on vacation.

CONSIDER THIS: God wants us to be examples of what it means to live a life of faith. When people see us, they should see so much joy, peace, and happiness that they will want what we have. Take an honest look at your life. Are you as happy as you know you should be deep down inside? If not, what is stealing your joy and causing you to get upset? Why are you worried? In the space below, name your worries specifically. For each matter that concerns you, identify at least one adjustment in your attitude or your behavior in relation to it that will retrain your mind for happiness.

Most people ask for happiness
on condition.
Happiness can be felt only
if you don't set any conditions.

—*Arthur Rubinstein*

_____

_____

_____

_____

_____   ❧

_____   The foolish person seeks
                                 happiness in the distance;
_____   the wise person grows it
                                 under his feet.
_____
                                 —*James Oppenheim*
_____

_____

_____

_____

_____

_____

WHAT THE SCRIPTURES SAY

May the righteous be glad
and rejoice before God;
may they be happy and joyful.
                    —*Psalm 68:3*

Rejoice in the Lord always; I will say it again: Rejoice!
                    —*Philippians 4:4*

A PRAYER FOR TODAY

Lord, this is the day that you have made. I will rejoice and be happy in it. I commit my worries and troubles to You. I choose to live in the joy that You have made possible. I thank You for all I have. Please help me to focus on the positive and leave the negative behind.

_____

_____

_____

_____

_____

_____

_____

_____

_____

_____

_____

_____

_____

_____

_____

_____

_____

TAKEAWAY TRUTH: I will step out of my doubts and step into faith. I will leave discouragement behind and live in joy.

DAY 4

GOD IN YOUR VIEW

KEY TRUTH: You can enjoy the "calm delight" of faith when you magnify your God instead of magnifying your problem.

Following the devastation of Hurricane Katrina, I was watching a special news program one day as reporters were interviewing people in New Orleans who had lived through it. Person after person told his or her story, and most of them were extremely negative and bitter, blaming other people, blaming the government, blaming God.

One young woman stepped up to the microphone, and I could tell immediately that she had a different attitude. She had a big smile, and her face almost seemed to glow. The reporter asked her somewhat sarcastically, "Okay, tell us your story. What's wrong?"

"Nothing's wrong," the woman said. "I'm not here to complain. I'm simply here to thank God that I'm still and alive and I have my health. I thank God that my children are okay."

The reporter was taken aback. Everyone else had been complaining about not having any electricity or water. It was more than a hundred degrees and they had no air-conditioning. He asked, "Well, what about your power? Your air-conditioning?"

She said, "I not only don't have any power, I don't even have my home. It was swept away in the flood." Then she smiled as she said, "I'll tell you what I do have. I have my hope, my joy, my peace. I know God is on my side."

That woman chose to take a heartrending, negative, unfortunate situation and turn it around; she stamped "positive" on it.

CONSIDER THIS: Happiness is not going to fall on you. It's a choice you have to make. Being positive doesn't necessarily come naturally. You have to make that decision daily. In the space below, write down at least ten positive thoughts with which you can start each day this week. Every morning, before you do anything else, read your positive thoughts and let them put a smile of faith on your face.

_____

_____

_____

_____

The word hope I take for faith;
and indeed hope is nothing else
but the constancy of faith.

—*John Calvin*

Sing songs for [God],
create beautiful things for Him,
give things up for Him, tell Him
what's on your mind and in your heart,
in general rejoice in Him and make
a fool of yourself for Him . . .

—*Frederick Buechner*

WHAT THE SCRIPTURES SAY

Glorify the LORD with me;
let us exalt His name together.
—*Psalm 34:3*

Shout for joy to the LORD, all the earth.
Worship the LORD with gladness;
come before him with joyful songs.
—*Psalm 100:1–2*

A PRAYER FOR TODAY

Father, I thank You that You have me at the right place at the right time. I am not going to be depressed. I am not going to worry. I believe You're directing my steps, and where You lead me is just where I should go. I will rejoice in You in every circumstance.

_____

_____

_____

_____

_____

_____

_____

_____

_____

_____

_____

_____

_____

_____

_____

_____

TAKEAWAY TRUTH: I will train my mind to see the good. I will get rid of any negative, conditioned responses and stamp what I see in my life as a "positive."

DAY 5

A WELL OF GOOD THINGS

KEY TRUTH: You can handle criticism if you refuse to take it personally, and in turn learn to celebrate the victories of others.

If you are going to become better, you will need to know how to deal with critics—people who are talking about you, judging you, or maybe even making false accusations. In the Old Testament times, these people were called "slingers." When an enemy attacked a city, their first priority was to pry the stones off the wall that was protecting that city. They would then sling those stones into the city's wells. The attackers knew if they could clog the wells with stones and interrupt the flow of water, eventually the people within the walls would have to come out.

Do you see the parallel? You have a well of good things on the inside, a well of joy, peace, and victory. Too often, we let the slingers clog up our wells. Perhaps somebody speaks derogatorily about you, but instead of letting it go, you dwell on it, growing more and more upset.

Make it a priority to keep your well pure. If somebody is critical of you, trying to show you in a bad light, recognize that is a stone coming your way. If you dwell on it, or get upset and vengeful, the person who threw that stone has accomplished his or her goal. Another stone landed in your well. Now your joy, peace, and victory have become more restricted. They don't flow as they should.

CONSIDER THIS: The way you overcome unwarranted criticism is by not allowing yourself to take revenge or even harboring an attitude that wants revenge. Don't sink to the accusers' level. Don't get defensive or try to prove that you're right and your critic is wrong. Keep your eyes on the prize; stay focused on your goals and do what you believe God wants you to do. In the space below, write out a statement of *your* prize, describing what God has given you to do. What gifts, talents, and resources has God given you? How will you use them this week?

_____

_____

_____

_____

_____

Praise can give criticism
the lead around the bend
and still win the race.

—*Bern Williams*

_____

_____

_____

_____

_____

_____

_____

_____

_____

_____

_____   ——————✂——————

_____   Sandwich every bit
of criticism between two layers
_____   of praise.

_____   —*Mary Kay Ash*

_____   _____

_____

_____

_____

_____

_____

WHAT THE SCRIPTURES SAY

If anyone will not welcome you or listen to your words, shake the dust off your feet when you leave that home or town.

—*Matthew 10:14*

But when the Jews opposed Paul and became abusive, he shook out his clothes in protest and said, "Your blood be on your own heads! I am clear of my responsibility."

—*Acts 18:6*

A PRAYER FOR TODAY

God, You have made me the person I am, and You are stirring up the good in me. Please help me to shake off any negativity that comes my way. Teach me to keep my eye on my goals and keep the flow of joy and peace and purity clear.

_____

_____

_____

_____

_____

_____

_____

_____

_____

_____

_____

_____

_____

_____

TAKEAWAY TRUTH: I will not be distracted by my critics. I realize that not everyone will agree with me, or cheer me on, but I will stay focused on using the gifts, talents, and resources God has given me.

DAY 6

RUN THE RACE

KEY TRUTH: Your destiny is not determined by your critics. You can rise above criticism by focusing your attention on running your own race.

A high school friend of mine was popular, fun, and outgoing, but he had an unusual high-pitched laugh. One day a couple of our friends started making fun of him, going around the school imitating his laugh. They didn't mean any harm. They were just teasing, trying to have fun. I noticed how that young man started to change, though. He quit laughing as much. He became much more quiet and reserved. Where he once was gregarious and the life of the party, little by little he tucked his true personality inside a shell. He lost his confidence, became insecure, and started overcompensating. That's what happens when we don't shake things off.

You may have some distinct features or personality traits. But know this: God made you like you are on purpose. If people are making fun of you or causing you to feel overly self-conscious, just shake it off. Don't let their comments or actions stick to you.

The other day I saw a parody that somebody produced about me speaking, and every time I smiled, my front teeth would *ping,* and a star would rise off my teeth, sort of like a toothpaste commercial. When I saw the parody, I laughed. I thought to myself,

That doesn't bother me one bit. I smile a lot. If somebody doesn't like it, I'll just smile some more.

CONSIDER THIS: You may have to endure some people speaking against you, but if you can stay on the high road and keep doing your best, you will prove their criticism invalid. Moreover, God will pour out His favor on you, in spite of your critics. In the space below, write a word portrait of yourself. Think of the God and Father who made you, who loves you and has a purpose for your life. How do you think He sees you?

_____

_____

_____

_____

> Never give in—in nothing,
> great or small, large or petty—
> except to convictions
> of honor and good sense.
>
> —*Winston Churchill*

_____

_____

_____

_____

_____

_____   ———————✸———————

_____

A leader who keeps his ear
to the ground allows his
rear end to become a target.

_____   —*Angie Papadakis*

_____   _____

_____

_____

_____

_____

_____

WHAT THE SCRIPTURES SAY

No weapon forged against you will prevail,
and you will refute every tongue that accuses you.

—*Isaiah 54:17*

Let us throw off everything that hinders and the sin that so easily
entangles, and let us run with perseverance the race marked out
for us.

—*Hebrews 12:1*

Do you not know that in a race all the runners run, but only one
gets the prize? Run in such a way as to get the prize.

—*1 Corinthians 9:24*

A PRAYER FOR TODAY

Father, thank You for Your favor, poured on me despite my critics. Help me to listen to Your voice and tune out the naysayers. Please give me the stamina to run my race for the prize. I look forward to what You have planned for me.

_____

_____

_____

_____

_____

_____

_____

_____

_____

_____

_____

_____

_____

_____

_____

_____

TAKEAWAY TRUTH: I will not allow the criticism of others to change me. I will keep my heart pure and stay true to who God has made me to be. Even when I'm tough on the outside, I'll remain tender on the inside.

DAY 7

RESPONSIBLE HAPPINESS

KEY TRUTH: God has not called you to be unhappy simply to keep somebody else happy.

I've found that high-maintenance people are usually controllers. They're not interested in you; they're interested in what you can do for them. They're interested in how you can make their life better. If you fall into the trap of trying to keep them happy, you're going to be weary and worn out, and you're going to be frustrated in your own life.

Many years ago, I attempted to help a married couple. They were fine people and I really liked them. In fact, when they moved to another state, I gave them some money and I tried to stay in touch. If they ever needed anything, I was always available. But it seemed like I was never doing enough. They were never happy.

I was being kind and generous, but they never saw any of that. They continually found some reason to complain, to find fault, or to make me feel guilty, as though I was not doing enough to help them.

One day I realized that they are high-maintenance people and I am not responsible for keeping them happy. I can't make them like me. I can't make them be grateful. I need to just run my race and not allow them to steal my joy.

I continued to be their friend, but I had to step back and let them work on making themselves happy. That made me very happy! That's a freeing way to live.

CONSIDER THIS: Too often, we live to please everybody else, but we neglect to take time to please ourselves. If you allow them, some people will draw all the time and energy right out of you. But if you dare to confront those people and start making the necessary changes, you will see your life go to a new level of happiness and you'll be free to fulfill the best plan that God has for you. Think about the people for whose happiness you have been taking responsibility. Name at least one below, then write down one change you can make that will set you free to be happy. Think about people who you've pressured into doing what you want. Name at least one below, then write down one positive change you can make to free yourself of the need to control them and give yourself the gift of happiness.

A man all wrapped up
in himself makes
a very small parcel.

—*BBC Radio*

_____

_____

_____

_____

_____

———————————————

> There is no happiness
> for people at the expense
> of other people.
>
> —*Anwar Sadat*

_____

_____

_____

_____

_____

_____

_____

WHAT THE SCRIPTURES SAY

"For whom am I toiling," he asked,
"and why am I depriving myself of enjoyment?"
—*Ecclesiastes 4:8*

So in everything, do to others what you would have them do to
you, for this sums up the Law and the Prophets.
—*Matthew 7:12*

A PRAYER FOR TODAY

Lord, You have designed me for a life that is full and satisfying. You have placed a call on my life that will allow me to experience the greatest happiness a person can feel. Help me to be wise enough to know the difference between Your plan for me to be generous and other people's controlling behavior to get what they want from me. Teach me to be kind without being manipulated. Let me love responsibly.

_____

_____

_____

_____

_____

_____

_____

_____

_____

_____

_____

_____

_____

TAKEAWAY TRUTH: I recognize that I am not responsible for the happiness of everybody around me. Today I will be aware that I am responsible for keeping myself happy. I will be kind to everyone around me, but I will not be manipulated. I will not take on a false sense of responsibility for the actions or attitudes of others.

STEP FIVE

Embrace the Place
Where You Are

DAY 1

FAITH TEACHES

KEY TRUTH: Faith doesn't always instantly deliver you, but it always carries you through.

The first year I went away to college, I applied for a job at the university television studio. The school owned a large, well-known production facility, and I'd always wanted to be a part of it. Television production was my passion. The first week of school, I met with the production manager in charge of all the cameramen and of hiring all the assistants. At that point, I had several years of camera experience under my belt.

The production manager went out of his way to be kind to me. He took a couple of hours to show me around, and we seemed to really hit it off. When it came time for me to leave, he said, "Joel, I'll call you later this week and I'll let you know about the job."

That week went by, and I didn't hear from him. Then another week and another. Finally I called him, and he was always busy or out of town. I didn't think I would have any problem getting that job, but the door simply wasn't opening. Worse yet, I wanted it so badly, but I could see it just wasn't meant to be. Finally I accepted it and embraced the thought: "No big deal. I'm just going to let it go."

God knows what's best for us. Although that job looked great to me at the time, I didn't know where God was taking me. Had I stayed there, I would have missed what God wanted me to do at Lakewood.

CONSIDER THIS: God is not going to remove every difficulty from you instantly. He uses those things to refine you, to do a fresh work in you. In the tough times, God develops your character. The fact is, we don't grow nearly as much when everything is easy; we grow when life is difficult, when we are exercising our spiritual muscles. Think back over your life experience so far. Remember a time when you didn't get your way. What door did God open for you? What blessings—for your well-being, your character, your relationships—did God bring about in your life? Describe the situation and the results below. Then identify one area in your life right now for which you are waiting for God's answer. Write it down. Then commit it to God in faith that He loves you and hears you and will answer in His time and His way.

_____

_____

_____

_____

_____

_____

_____

_____

_____

_____

_____

_____

_____   ———————⊗———————

_____   Faith is like radar that sees
                                          through the fog—the reality
_____   of things at a distance that
                                          the human eye cannot see.
_____
                                          —*Corrie ten Boom*
_____

_____   ———————————————

_____

_____

_____

_____

WHAT THE SCRIPTURES SAY

> Trust in the LORD with all your heart
> and lean not on your own understanding;
> in all your ways acknowledge him,
> and he will make your paths straight.
> > —*Proverbs 3:5–6*

For we also have had the gospel preached to us, just as they did; but the message they heard was of no value to them, because those who heard did not combine it with faith. Now we who have believed enter that rest.

> > —*Hebrews 4:2–3*

A PRAYER FOR TODAY

God, not my will, but Your will be done. Open up the right doors and close the wrong doors. Give me the vision to stay open to your direction and follow my heart as You lead it. I thank You, Lord, that You know what's best for me. I thank You that You are merciful and don't always give me my way. I pray that You'll teach me to trust You even when I don't understand.

_____

_____

_____

All I have seen teaches me
to trust the Creator
for all I have not seen.

—*Ralph Waldo Emerson*

TAKEAWAY TRUTH: I know that God works where there is an attitude of faith and expectancy. I will turn my situation over to God. I will not allow myself to worry or become frustrated. I will recognize that God is working behind the scenes, even when I cannot see external evidence of positive change.

DAY 2

RESTING IN TRUST

KEY TRUTH: It is in the difficult times that you grow stronger. That's when God is developing your character and preparing you for promotion. When you're at peace, you have power. When you're at rest, God can fight your battles for you.

I used to play basketball with my friends several times a week. One night after the game, it was still rather early, so I asked one of the guys if he wanted to stop and get something to eat. He casually answered, "No, Joel, I've got to go up to the hospital. I'm taking chemotherapy."

"You've got to be kidding!" I said. "You're doing what?"

"This is my second bout with cancer," he replied, "so I take chemo three times a week."

I was amazed. I didn't even know anything was wrong with him. He always had a smile on his face, always was upbeat and had an attitude of faith. He looked as if he were on top of the world.

Other people in similar situations drag around, wallowing in self-pity, defeated and blaming God. But not him. He knew that God was still in control. Even though he didn't like his circumstances, even though he was uncomfortable, he didn't allow it to get him down. He dealt with it and moved on. Several years later, he's cancer-free. God has totally healed him.

CONSIDER THIS: God wants you to remain at rest, to keep your peace of mind. As long as we're upset, frustrated, and all bent out of shape, God will back away and wait. To show God that you are trusting Him, you must stay in peace; keep a smile on your face; have a good attitude day in and day out. You may be fighting some serious battles, but the good news is, God is bigger than anything that you're facing.

In the space below, write out the hard things that you're dealing with one at a time. At the end of each, declare your trust by writing, "Lord, I commit this to you."

_____

_____

_____

_____

_____

When peace like a river attendeth my way,
when sorrows like sea billows roll,
whatever my lot, You have taught me to say,
It is well, it is well with my soul.

—*Horatio Spafford*

_____

_____

_____

_____   ❧

_____   We must accept
                                finite disappointment,
_____   but we must never lose
                                  infinite hope.
_____
                                —*Rev. Martin Luther King Jr.*
_____

_____

_____

_____

_____

_____

_____

WHAT THE SCRIPTURES SAY

Cast your cares on the LORD
and he will sustain you;
he will never let the righteous fall.
—*Psalm 55:22*

Humble yourselves, therefore, under God's mighty hand, that he
may lift you up in due time. Cast all your anxiety on him because
he cares for you.

—*1 Peter 5:6–7*

A PRAYER FOR TODAY

Father, please give me the strength to go through every trial with a good attitude. Help me to keep my joy. Help me to keep my peace. I'm trusting You. I know You can do what men can't do, and I'm committing my life into Your hands.

_____

_____

_____

_____

_____

_____

_____

_____

_____

_____

_____

_____

_____

_____

_____

TAKEAWAY TRUTH: I can trust God no matter what my circumstances. I will give the battle to Him and rest assured that He will take care of me. God is in control, and He can give me the strength to endure anything.

DAY 3

JOYFUL IN HOPE

KEY TRUTH: God wants you to learn to have peace in the midst of the storms so you can experience His best in your life.

Throughout Scripture, the person who truly trusts in God is compared to an eagle. The eagle has some pests, one of which is the crow. He's always squawking, always causing the eagle trouble. The truth is we all have a few crows in our life. You may have an entire flock of them, along with a few chickens and turkeys as well!

Certain people can rub us the wrong way; they can irritate us if we allow them to. We need to take a lesson from the eagle instead. When the eagle is out flying, often a crow will come up right behind him and start to pester him, aggravating and annoying him. Although the eagle is much larger, he cannot maneuver quickly. To get rid of his pest, the eagle simply stretches out his eight-foot wingspan and catches some of the thermal currents, and he rises up higher and higher. Eventually, he gets to an altitude where no other bird can live. The crow can't even breathe up there. On rare occasions, eagles have been spotted at altitudes as high as 20,000 feet, nearly as high as a jet flies.

If you want to get rid of your pests, you need to rise higher. Don't sink down to the opposition's level. Be the bigger person.

Overlook their faults. Walk in love and dare to bless even you~~~
enemies. In the long run, crows can't compete with eagles.

CONSIDER THIS: You are an eagle, made in the image of the
Almighty God. The turkeys, chickens, and crows cannot live at the
altitude for which you were designed to soar. God is in complete
control of your life. He's promised that if you will remain at rest,
He'll make your wrongs right. He'll bring justice into your life.
You don't have to worry, nor must you be controlled by your circumstances. You can do as the eagle and rise up above. What are
the turkeys, chickens, and crows in your life right now? Write
about them in the space below, then describe yourself, rising like
the eagle you are above the temptations to pay back, to worry, to
argue or turn cold.

Sometimes our fate resembles
a fruit tree in winter.
Who would think that those
branches would turn green
again and blossom,
but we hope it, we know it.

—*Johann Wolfgang von Goethe*

There are no hopeless situations;
there are only people who have
grown hopeless about them.

—Clare Boothe Luce

WHAT THE SCRIPTURES SAY

But those who hope in the LORD
will renew their strength.
They will soar on wings like eagles;
they will run and not grow weary,
they will walk and not be faint.

—Isaiah 40:31

Be joyful in hope, patient in affliction, faithful in prayer.

—Romans 12:12

A PRAYER FOR TODAY

God, I trust you. I know You are bigger than my problems. I know You are bigger than my struggles. I know You are bigger than my enemies. I know most of all that You are in control. I can trust You to fight my battles for me.

_____

_____

_____

_____

_____

_____

_____

_____

_____

_____

_____

_____

_____

_____

_____

_____

TAKEAWAY TRUTH: God is on my side. There's nothing too difficult for Him. I won't be a crow or a chicken. I'll be the eagle God made me to be.

DAY 4

THE GIFT OF MEMORY

KEY TRUTH: One of the best ways to build your faith is to constantly remember what God has done for you.

In the Old Testament, God commanded His people to celebrate certain feasts so they would not forget what He had done for them, and so they could pass on those inspiring stories to the next generation. Several times a year, the Israelites stopped whatever they were doing and everybody celebrated how God brought them out of slavery, or how God defeated this enemy, or how He protected them against that calamity. These celebrations were not optional; they were commanded, and the people were required to attend and remember God's goodness to them.

In other places, the Bible records how God's people put down "memorial stones." These large markers were to remind the people of specific victories God had given them. Every time they or future generations passed by a memorial, they would remember the mighty things God had done.

You can take time to remember your victories, and celebrate what God has done in your life. Remember when God made a way for you when it looked as if there was no way. Remember when you were so lonely, and God brought somebody special into your life. Recall how God has healed you or someone you know.

CONSIDER THIS: When we learn to recall the good things God has done, it helps us to stay in an attitude of faith and to remain grateful. It's hard to go around complaining when you are constantly thinking about how good God has been to you. It's hard to get negative and to veer off into unbelief when you are always talking about God's blessings and favor in your life. What has God been doing in your life? Use the space below to create a memorial to the mighty things God has done for you. List at least ten specific instances of God's great blessings. The more you practice noticing and remembering God's good work, the more it will become a deep-down part of you.

_____

_____

_____

_____

The more we count
the blessings we have,
the less we crave
the luxuries we haven't.

—*William A. Ward*

_____

_____

_____

_____

_____

_____

_____

_____

_____

_____

_____

_____

_____

_____

_____

_____

_____

_____

_____

What is memory?
Not a storehouse,
not a trunk in the attic,
but an instrument that constantly
refines the past into a narrative,
accessible and acceptable
to oneself.

—*Stanley Kauffmann*

WHAT THE SCRIPTURES SAY

Look to the LORD and his strength;
seek his face always.
Remember the wonders he has done,
his miracles, and the judgments he pronounced.
> —*1 Chronicles 16:11–12*

I will remember the deeds of the LORD;
yes, I will remember your miracles of long ago.
I will meditate on all your works
and consider all your mighty deeds.
> —*Psalm 77:11–12*

A PRAYER FOR TODAY

Lord, I remember Your great goodness to me. I know that You chose me before the foundations of the world, and that You provide for me each day of my life. I believe that the good You have done in the past, You will do in the present and in the future. I pray that You will keep my memory strong and tuned to You all the time.

_____

_____

_____

_____

_____

_____

_____

_____

_____

_____

_____

_____

_____

_____

TAKEAWAY TRUTH: I will look for glimpses of God's goodness in the little things of my life. I will be more aware of His work in the ordinary areas of life—a kind word from a stranger, a rainbow in the sky, a bird perched on my windowsill, a flower blooming in a field.

DAY 5

TALKING TO YOURSELF

KEY TRUTH: There is no such thing as a coincidence when your life is directed by God. When something good happens to you, be sensitive, recognize the work of God, and learn to recall it often.

Shortly after Victoria and I were married, I was driving on a Houston freeway by myself. It was a Monday afternoon, and it had been pouring down rain for nearly twenty minutes. I was driving in the second lane from the left, and when I changed lanes I sloshed through a large puddle of water. My tires lost traction and the car hydroplaned. I lost control of the car and headed straight toward the median strip traveling at a speed of about fifty miles per hour. When I hit the barrier, it catapulted me back across the freeway and spun my car violently out of control.

As I spun back across the highway, I found myself looking straight into the headlights of an oncoming eighteen-wheeler. It looked like I could reach out and touch his grill. I closed my eyes, expecting to hear the crunch of metal at any moment, assuming my life was over.

Somehow, someway, however, I suddenly found myself in the ditch on the other side of the freeway. I had crossed six lanes of traffic during rush hour in Houston, Texas, and no other vehicle had crashed into me! I noticed that the driver of the truck that had almost hit me had pulled over. When he backed up to where I was, the driver bounded out of the truck's cab. "Boy, you must be living right!" he said. "I don't know how I missed you. I know this sounds odd, but right at the last moment, I felt this pocket of wind push me into the other lane." He thought it was a pocket of wind. I knew it was the angel of the Lord.

CONSIDER THIS: When something happens in your life that you know is God, write it down. When you know God opened up a door, or spared your life, or spoke to you a specific word of direction, or quickened a Scripture in your heart and lifted your spirits—write it down. Keep a running record of the good things that God has done for you. In the space below, start right now. Think back over the past days and months. Remember what God has been doing in your life and start the habit of keeping a record of it.

_____

_____

> Talk to yourself about your own life . . .
> Talk to yourself about what matters
> most to you, because if you don't,
> you may forget what matters
> most to you.
>
> —*Frederick Buechner I*

> Writing down is a form of the incarnation of God's Word. It becomes tangible, visible, and concrete. It forces us to be precise, definite, and particular.
>
> —*Walter Trobisch*

WHAT THE SCRIPTURES SAY

Remember that you were slaves in Egypt and that the LORD your God brought you out of there with a mighty hand and an outstretched arm.

—*Deuteronomy 5:15*

Great are the works of the LORD;
they are pondered by all who delight in them.
—*Psalm 111:2*

A PRAYER FOR TODAY

Lord, the works of Your Hand in my life are great. You have loved me, guided me, restored me, and healed me. In all the important moments, You are there. In all the precious details, You are there. Teach me to see, I pray, and help me to remember Your watchfulness over me.

_____

_____

_____

_____

_____

_____

_____

_____

_____

_____

_____

_____

_____

_____

_____

TAKEAWAY TRUTH: I will keep a notebook of all the great things God has done in my life. God is holding me in the palm of His hand, and He will take care of me. When I'm tempted to get discouraged or defeated, I'll read my record of His love and care.

DAY 6

BACKSTAGE MIRACLES

KEY TRUTH: You can rest and enjoy God's peace when you remember and trust that God is working behind the scenes in your life, even when you don't see anything happening.

The fact is we all have difficulties; we all have things in life that can steal our joy, steal our peace. We have to learn to turn them over to God. You may be trying to figure everything out, trying to solve every problem. But it would take so much pressure off you, and you would enjoy your life so much more, if you could just learn to relinquish control and start believing that God really is directing your steps.

The Bible reminds us, "For it is God who is all the while at work in you." Notice, God doesn't work for a while, then go off on a two- or three-year vacation, and then come back and work a little more. God is constantly at work in your life. That means that although you may not be able to see it, God is arranging things in your favor. He is getting the right people lined up to come across your path. He is creating solutions to problems you haven't even considered yet. God is constantly working behind the scenes in your life.

CONSIDER THIS: You don't know what God is doing behind the scenes. Don't get discouraged just because you don't see anything happening. That doesn't mean God is not working. In fact, many times God works most when we see it the least. It is a test of our faith. We have to dig in our heels and show God what we're made of. In the space below, write a list of the things you know about God's love and care. Find the Scriptures that talk about the way He loves us. Read about His qualities and characteristics and write them down. If this is the God of your life, what do you have to fear?

_____

_____

_____

_____

_____

_____

It is by logic that we prove,
but by intuition that
we discover.

—*Henri Poincaré*

_____

_____

_____

_____   ———————⧜———————

_____   Some things have to be
                                            believed to be seen.
_____
                                            —*Ralph Hodgson*
_____
                                            ——————————————
_____

_____

_____

_____

_____

WHAT THE SCRIPTURES SAY

> Trust in the LORD with all your heart
> and lean not on your own understanding;
> in all your ways acknowledge him,
> and he will make your paths straight.
>   —*Proverbs 3:5–6*

And we also thank God continually because, when you received the word of God, which you heard from us, you accepted it not as the word of men, but as it actually is, the word of God, which is at work in you who believe.

—*1 Thessalonians 2:13*

A PRAYER FOR TODAY

Father, I'm trusting You. I believe that You are in control. And even though I may not see anything tangible happening, I believe You are working in my life, going before me, making my crooked places straight, and causing me to be at the right place at the right time.

_____

_____

_____

_____

_____

_____

_____

_____

_____

_____

_____

_____

_____

TAKEAWAY TRUTH: I will remember that God has already pre-arranged a bright future for me. I will trust in the truth that He is fighting my battles for me, getting everything arranged in my favor. I will put my stressed-out living behind me because God is orchestrating everything behind the scenes.

DAY 7

GOD IN THE DETAILS

KEY TRUTH: You can trust God even in the small things in your life.

The den of the town house in which my parents once lived had large windows that looked out onto the courtyard. Birds flitted back and forth between the trees in the yard. One bird in particular became a favorite of my mother's. Every day a beautiful little cardinal would perch on one of the branches right by the window. My mother enjoyed having it there. She got to the point where she looked forward to seeing it each day. Like clockwork, the little bird showed up and spent the afternoon in the courtyard. This went on for five or six months, but eventually the friendly little bird quit coming by. I tried to give my mother my pet hamster to console her, but she didn't want that!

About a year later, my father went to be with the Lord. Now Mother was at home by herself. She had to make some adjustments. I'm sure at times she was tempted to be lonely, tempted to get down and discouraged.

Then one day, the little cardinal came back. To some people, that may have been coincidence, or merely an explainable function of nature. But to my mother and our family, that was God saying, "I still have a plan. I'm still in control."

CONSIDER THIS: The little signs in our lives are simply glimpses that God gives us to build our faith. They are reminders He is working behind the scenes. Our responsibility is to be sensitive to His leading, to be on the lookout for His hand moving in our everyday circumstances. If you are tuned in to God, you will soon recognize that most of the time, you didn't simply bump into somebody. You didn't just get a lucky break. You didn't just happen to be at the right place at the right time. God has been directing your steps.

Think about the path you've traveled in the last week. Think about the details, the people you talked to, the challenges you faced, the little things that affected you as you lived your life. As you think back, what glimpses can you discover of God's goodness to you? Were there "coincidences"? Did something happen at just the right moment? Did you face something that made you put your faith to the test? In the space below, record the ways in which you can sense that God blessed you in your life this week.

_____

_____

———— ❧ ————   _____

_____

_____

God's presence is so much   _____
beyond the human experience
of being together that it quite   _____
easily is perceived as absence.
_____
—Henri Nouwen
_____

_____   _____

_____

_____

_____

_____

_____

_____

_____

_____

_____

_____ We praise God not to celebrate
our own faith but to give thanks
_____ for the faith God has in us.

—*Kathleen Norris*

_____

_____

_____

_____

_____

_____

WHAT THE SCRIPTURES SAY

If I rise on the wings of the dawn,
if I settle on the far side of the sea,
even there your hand will guide me,
your right hand will hold me fast.

—*Psalm 139:9–10*

Are not two sparrows sold for a penny? Yet not one of them will
fall to the ground apart from the will of your Father. And even the
very hairs of your head are all numbered. So don't be afraid; you
are worth more than many sparrows.

—*Matthew 10:29–31*

A PRAYER FOR TODAY

God, I praise You and thank You for loving Your children so much that You dwell in our details. You know all that we suffer, all that we doubt and fear, and You show Yourself to us in a million small graces every day. Please give me eyes to see and a heart to respond to Your intimate love.

_____

_____

_____

_____

_____

_____

_____

_____

_____

_____

_____

_____

_____

_____

_____

_____

_____

TAKEAWAY TRUTH: I will dare to trust God today. I will dare to believe that even in my disappointments, heartaches, and pains, God is right here with me. He said He would never leave me or forsake me. I may not know what my future holds, but I know who holds my future.

STEP SIX

Develop Your Inner Life

DAY 1

THE STILL, SMALL VOICE

KEY TRUTH: We need to listen to the still, small voice of God's promptings. God knows what's best for us.

God has given us our own free will. He will not force us to do what is right. He won't force us to make good decisions. It's up to each one of us individually to pay attention to the still, small voice; at the same time, we mustn't get so busy or self-directed that we miss what God is trying to tell us. We must learn to act on His leading.

God's directions often affect the most practical aspects of our lives. Recently, a young woman told me that she felt a strong urge to go to the doctor to get a medical checkup. She looked as healthy as could be, was active and energetic, and exercised regularly. Nevertheless, the feeling persisted: "Go see the doctor. Go get a checkup." That still, small voice was speaking to her. For several weeks, she ignored it and put it off. "Oh, I'm fine. That's not a message for me."

But she couldn't get away from it. She finally decided to schedule an appointment with her doctor. During a routine checkup, the doctor discovered a small cyst in her body and found that it was malignant. Thankfully, he was able to remove it completely, because it hadn't spread. The young woman required no further treatment. But after the operation, the doctor told her, "It's a good thing you came in when you did, because a couple of years later, this could have been a major problem, possibly even life-threatening."

CONSIDER THIS: Anytime you obey, a blessing will follow. Why? Because you are sowing a seed to grow and rise higher. It may not happen overnight, but at some point, in some way, you will see God's goodness in your life to a greater measure. Isn't it amazing that we can know the right thing to do, yet still ignore it? Don't let that be you. Be obedient now, so you won't have regrets later on. Is God speaking to you now? Is there a still, small voice telling you that something in your life is just not right? Use the space below to describe God's prompting that you have ignored so far. Or maybe you've listened and obeyed. In that case, describe what you heard and how you responded.

Conscience is that still, small voice that is sometimes too loud for comfort.

—*Bert Murray*

_____

_____

_____

_____

_____

_____   ❧

_____   To be brought to the place
                      where we can hear the call
_____   of God is to be profoundly
                      changed.
_____
                      —*Oswald Chambers*
_____

_____

_____

_____

_____

_____

WHAT THE SCRIPTURES SAY

Today, if you hear his voice,
do not harden your hearts.
Psalm 95:7–8

See to it, brothers, that none of you has a sinful, unbelieving heart that turns away from the living God. . . . We have come to share in Christ if we hold firmly till the end the confidence we had at first.

—*Hebrews 3:12, 14*

A PRAYER FOR TODAY

Father, I believe that You have a high calling for me. Please help me hear Your voice when my conscience speaks. Please give me strength to deal with the issues You bring to light in my life. Deliver me from complacency so I can keep rising higher.

_____

_____

_____

_____

_____

_____

_____

_____

_____

_____

_____

_____

_____

_____

TAKEAWAY TRUTH: Today I will be aware of the issues God brings to light in my life, and I will be quick to obey and make the necessary changes. I will pay more attention to my conscience, that still, small voice within.

DAY 2

A STEP AT A TIME

KEY TRUTH: When you ask for forgiveness, God can restore you. That's when He'll put you back on your best path.

When King David committed adultery with Bathsheba, he tried to cover it up. Making matters worse, he sent Bathsheba's husband to the front lines of the battle and then ordered his general to pull back, resulting in certain death. For one full year, David pretended that everything was okay; he went on with life and business. No doubt, he thought, *If I don't deal with it, if I ignore it, it won't bother me; it won't affect me.*

That year was one of the worst of David's life. He was miserable. The Scripture says he was also weak; he grew sick physically and had all kinds of problems. That is what happens when we refuse to deal with things. We step out of God's protection and favor. When we live with a guilty conscience, we don't feel good about ourselves, so we take it out on other people. Many times, just like David, we're weak, defeated, living in mediocrity. It's because of the poison on the inside.

After a year of living in denial, King David finally admitted his sin and his mistakes after a prophet confronted him about his misdeeds. David said, "God, I'm sorry. Please forgive me. Create in me a clean heart. Restore the joy of my salvation." When

David sincerely did that, God restored him. David got his joy, peace, and victory back, and although he had failed miserably, he went on to do great things.

CONSIDER THIS: Anything that God asks you to do is for your benefit. It's so He can ultimately release more of His favor in your life. Moreover, anything God asks of you, He always gives you the grace to do. If you will take that step of faith, God's grace will be there to help you. In the space below, describe the character you know God wants to blossom in you. What obstacles do you face? Describe yourself on the victorious side of moving beyond them.

_____

_____

_____

_____

A gem is not polished without rubbing, nor a man perfected without trials.

—*Chinese proverb*

❦

Real religion is a way of life, not a white cloak to be wrapped around us on the Sabbath and then cast aside into the six-day closet of unconcern.

—*William Arthur Ward*

WHAT THE SCRIPTURES SAY

From everyone who has been given much, much will be demanded; and from the one who has been entrusted with much, much more will be asked.

—*Luke 12:48*

Live as children of light (for the fruit of the light consists in all goodness, righteousness and truth) and find out what pleases the Lord.

—*Ephesians 5:8–10*

A PRAYER FOR TODAY

God, I know that You provide all I need to be my best self. I ask your forgiveness for all the ways in which I forget your sufficient grace. Please empower me to step out in faith, knowing that You will not trip me up. Please help me to obey, knowing that when I obey, You will take me farther than I can even imagine.

_____

_____

_____

_____

_____

_____

_____

_____

_____

_____

_____

_____

_____

_____

_____

_____

_____

TAKEAWAY TRUTH: I know God has great things in store for me. I won't settle for mediocrity, bad habits, or bad attitudes. I will deal with the issues God brings to light and learn to obey quickly.

DAY 3

A TENDER CONSCIENCE

KEY TRUTH: Respect your conscience so God can use it to help lead you and keep you out of trouble.

Recently, I met a man whose family lives in another country while he has been in the United States for several years working with his company. He told me how he came to be intimately involved with another woman. They have been in a relationship for a couple of years, but he feels guilty about it. He said, "Joel, I just feel terrible. I know that this relationship is not right. I really want to change, but I just can't seem to do it."

"You are in an interesting situation," I told him. "You are the exception to the rule, because most people who have been overriding their consciences that long no longer care. They don't feel anything. They're not concerned."

"What do you think I should do?" he asked.

"First of all, you should thank God that you still have a tender conscience and be grateful that you still have that concern." I then challenged him to make the necessary changes before that uneasiness wore off.

Don't make the mistake of overriding your conscience. Respect it. Just as you respect your boss or someone else with authority over you, learn to treat your conscience in the same way. When you're about to do something that is not beneficial or something that will get you into trouble, your conscience causes you to feel uneasy. Don't ignore that warning.

CONSIDER THIS: Your conscience tries to keep you out of trouble. It's God trying to warn you. Too many times we ignore it and choose to do our own thing. Understand, every time you ignore your conscience, the next time that voice will speak more softly. Unfortunately, you can get to the place where you have totally drowned out the voice of your conscience. In the space below, recall a time in the past when you chose to ignore your conscience. Describe what happened, how you felt, what the consequences were. Then answer this question: What might have happened if you had listened to your conscience? How would your life be different? Describe how you might better respond to a similar situation today.

There is no pillow so soft
as a clear conscience.

—*French proverb*

_____

_____

_____

_____

_____

_____

_____   ⸎

Conscience is God's
_____   presence in man.

_____   —*Emanuel Swedenborg*

_____

_____

_____

_____

_____

_____

WHAT THE SCRIPTURES SAY

Hate what is evil; cling to what is good. . . . Never be lacking in
zeal, but keep your spiritual fervor, serving the Lord.

—*Romans 12:9, 11*

I give you this instruction in keeping with the prophecies once
made about you, so that by following them you may fight the
good fight, holding on to faith and a good conscience.

—*1 Timothy 1:18–19*

A PRAYER FOR TODAY

God, help me to stay sensitive to Your voice. Don't let me get calloused, cold, or numb in any area of my life, in my attitude, or in how I treat people, or in what I say or what I do. God, help me to have a tender conscience.

_____

_____

_____

_____

_____

_____

_____

_____

_____

_____

_____

_____

_____

_____

_____

TAKEAWAY TRUTH: I will learn to be sensitive. I will stop when my conscience says stop. I will pay attention to what I'm feeling inside and obey instead of overriding my conscience.

DAY 4

TRUST AND OBEY

KEY TRUTH: God rewards obedience.

A young man with whom I attended college had a habit of being short with people. Sometimes, he was downright rude. One day we were at a restaurant together with a group of guys from the school, and the waiter mixed up my friend's order. My friend jumped down the waiter's throat. I mean, he let him have it and embarrassed him in front of all of us.

About an hour after we got back to the dorm, my friend came into my room and asked if he could borrow my car. I said, "Sure you can, but where are you going at this late hour?"

"Joel, I feel terrible," he said. "I treated that waiter so badly, I can't even sleep. I'm going to go back there and apologize to him."

That young man changed over the course of that year. He went from being hard, cold, and rude to being one of the kindest, most considerate people you could ever meet. God will help you to change, if you simply work with Him.

None of us is perfect. We all make mistakes, but we can learn to obey our own consciences if we can be big enough to say, "I'm sorry, I didn't treat you right, I'll do better next time."

CONSIDER THIS: If you will be sensitive and maintain a clear conscience, there's no limit to what God will do in your life. In contrast, when you have a guilty conscience, you don't feel good about yourself. You're not happy; you can't pray with boldness; you feel condemned. You don't expect good things, and you usually don't receive them. The best thing you can do is go back and make things right. When you do that, your conscience will relax, and God will help you to do better next time.

It's important to remember that it's never too late to do the right thing. When was the last time you examined your conscience to make sure that you were listening and obeying? Right now, take some time to be quiet and hear the still, small voice within you. In the space below, record all the things that continue to clutter your conscience and steal your peace and joy. After each one, write out what you can do to make it right.

_____

_____

Many people feel "guilty" about things they shouldn't feel guilty about, in order to shut out feelings of guilt about things they should feel guilty about.

—*Sydney J. Harris*

_____

_____

_____   —————— ✥ ——————

_____   A good conscience

_____   is a continual Christmas.

_____   —*Ben Franklin*

_____   ————————————

_____

_____

_____

_____

_____

_____

WHAT THE SCRIPTURES SAY

But love your enemies, do good to them, and lend to them without expecting to get anything back. Then your reward will be great, and you will be sons of the Most High, because he is kind to the ungrateful and wicked.

—*Luke 6:35*

Serve wholeheartedly, as if you were serving the Lord, not men, because you know that the Lord will reward everyone for whatever good he does.

—*Ephesians 6:7–8*

A PRAYER FOR TODAY

God, I'm sorry. Please forgive me for the ways in which I've ignored that still, small voice that You've placed within me. Right now, I pray that You'll bring to my mind those things in my life that still need to be made right. I ask that You'll give me the courage to obey and the grace to do better next time.

_____

_____

_____

_____

_____

_____

_____

_____

_____

_____

_____

_____

_____

TAKEAWAY TRUTH: God does not expect me to change overnight. He wants me to keep making progress. He will lead me as I listen to my conscience and live an obedient life, and His blessings will chase me down and overtake me.

DAY 5

THE CLEAN SLATE

KEY TRUTH: If your conscience is clear, life is good.

Many people are living with a heaviness hanging over their lives. They have a nagging feeling; something's always bothering them. They're not happy. The problem is they don't have a clear conscience. They've ignored the warnings for too long. They've gotten hard and cold in certain areas.

That sensitivity won't change until you make the proper adjustments. If there are things that you are doing that you know you should not be doing, then make some adjustments. Or if there are things that you *should* be doing and you're not, then make those changes. As I've said, it may not be something big. You may not be living in some sordid sin, but maybe God is dealing with you about having a better attitude, about spending more time with your children, about eating healthier. Whatever it is, make a decision that you're going to pay more attention to your conscience and that you are going to be quick to obey. That's when the heaviness will leave. I like what the Apostle Paul said in *Acts 23.* He said, "I have always lived before God with a clear conscience." That should be our goal as well.

CONSIDER THIS: When our conscience is clear, condemnation flees. When we have a clear conscience, we can be happy. Other people may try to judge us or condemn us, but negative input will bounce right off us. I know I'm not perfect, but I also know this: My conscience is clear before God. I know I'm doing my best to please Him. That's why I can sleep well at night. That's why I can lie down in peace. That's why I have a smile on my face.

Consider your lifestyle, your daily habits, your day-to-day choices. Are there aspects of your everyday life that trouble your peace? Are there choices that are silently condemning you day after day? List them below. After each one, describe how you can improve in obedience to God. What will obedience look like? What will you do?

_____

_____

_____

_____

_____

Self-discipline is when your conscience tells you to do something and you don't talk back.

—*W. K. Hope*

_____

_____

_____

_____   ———————— ✤ ————————

_____   A long habit of not thinking a
                                        thing wrong gives it a superficial
_____   appearance of being right.

_____   —*Thomas Paine*

_____   _____

_____

_____

WHAT THE SCRIPTURES SAY

> Search me, O God, and know my heart;
> test me and know my anxious thoughts.
> See if there is any offensive way in me,
> and lead me in the way everlasting.
> —*Psalm 139:23–24*

Therefore, as God's chosen people, holy and dearly loved, clothe yourselves with compassion, kindness, humility, gentleness and patience. Bear with each other and forgive whatever grievances you may have against one another. Forgive as the Lord forgave you. And over all these virtues put on love, which binds them all together in perfect unity. Let the peace of Christ rule in your hearts.

—*Colossians 3:12–15*

A PRAYER FOR TODAY

Lord, thank You for giving me a conscience that can guide me into Your peace and joy. I've made mistakes, but You promise that when I confess and repent, You are faithful to forgive me. I can be weak, but You promise that Your strength is sufficient for me. I praise You for the good life ahead that follows a clear conscience.

_____

_____

_____

_____

_____

_____

_____

_____

_____

_____

_____

_____

_____

TAKEAWAY TRUTH: Today I will be aware of the issues that I have ignored for so long. I'll make my conscience newly tender so I can be aware as God brings other issues to light in my life, and I will be quick to obey and make the necessary changes so I can move up higher.

DAY 6

DIGGING DEEP

KEY TRUTH: Only as you get to the root and start dealing with the source of the problem can you realistically expect positive changes.

I heard about a man who owned a bunch of horses, and one day one of the horses kicked a wooden fence and scraped his leg badly. The owner took the horse to his barn, cleaned the wound, and bandaged the animal's leg. A few weeks later, the man noticed that the horse was still bothered by that bruise. The owner called a veterinarian to come examine the horse. After checking the animal, the vet prescribed some antibiotics.

Almost immediately, the horse responded positively to the medication and began to do much better. A month or two went by, however, and the owner noticed that the injury still had not healed; it actually appeared to be worse than ever. So the vet put the horse back on antibiotics.

Once again the animal responded and was fine for a few weeks, but the process repeated itself. The wound simply would not heal. Finally, the owner loaded up the horse and took him down to the veterinarian's clinic. He knew he had to find out why this wound wouldn't heal. In the clinic, the veterinarian put the horse under anesthesia and began to probe the injured leg. Once he got deep enough, the vet discovered a large sliver of wood that had gone far below the skin when the horse had hit the fence many months previously. The vet realized that every time the horse went off the antibiotic, the infection caused by that foreign object returned. They had been treating the symptoms rather than treating the true source of the horse's pain.

CONSIDER THIS: It's good when we try to improve, but so often we don't deal with the real source of the problem. No matter how much we want to be better, the issue just keeps coming back, and we can't seem to get free.

It is usually easier to make excuses for our behavior, to pass the blame and try to justify our behavior. But if we want to experience God's best, we must learn to take responsibility for our thoughts, words, attitudes, and actions. For lasting, positive change, we must go deeper and not merely look at what we do. What is the issue that most plagues you? Write it down in the space below. Then answer these questions: What is the root of this problem? Why do I act this way? Why am I out of control in this area?

_____

_____

A man cannot be comfortable   _____

without his own approval.   _____

—*Mark Twain*   _____

_____

_____

_____

_____   ⚜

_____   A lot of people mistake a short
                                    memory for a clear conscience.
_____
                                         —*Mark Larson*
_____

_____   _____

_____

_____

_____

_____

_____

_____

_____

WHAT THE SCRIPTURES SAY

But everything exposed by the light becomes visible, for it is light
that makes everything visible. This is why it is said:
"Wake up, O sleeper,
rise from the dead,
and Christ will shine on you."

—*Ephesians 5:13–14*

Nothing in all creation is hidden from God's sight. Everything is
uncovered and laid bare before the eyes of him to whom we must
give account.

—*Hebrews 4:13*

A PRAYER FOR TODAY

Father, You know so much more about me than I do. Please help me get to the bottom of my bad choices and poor judgments. Nothing is hidden from You, so I ask that You'll show me the deep issues that I have not uncovered. I pray that You'll give me the courage it takes to go deeper, be honest, and change.

_____

_____

_____

_____

———————————❦———————————   _____

_____

It is only with the heart that one   _____
can see rightly; what is essential   _____
is invisible to the eye.   _____

—*Antoine de Saint-Exupéry*   _____

_____

_____

_____

_____

_____

_____

TAKEAWAY TRUTH: I will stop focusing only on the surface issues in my life. Instead, I'll look inside and get honest with myself. This week, I'll commit myself to dealing with the bad root that is producing bad fruit in my life.

DAY 7

NO PAIN, NO GAIN

KEY TRUTH: The pain of change is much less than the pain of staying in mediocrity.

Not long ago, a man told me that whenever he took time to enjoy his life, he felt guilty about it. He felt condemned, as though he were doing something wrong. Over the years, he engrossed himself in his work. He became a workaholic, not taking any time for himself, not taking any time for his family. Ironically, his overworking was all because of these feelings of guilt. His life was out of balance. This went on year after year until one day he decided to get honest and let God in that room of his heart. He said, "God, why do I feel this way? Why do I feel guilt when I just want to go out and have fun, to enjoy being with my family?"

He remembered that as he was growing up his father was extremely strict. He came from a military family, and his dad didn't allow any fun in the house. Everything was serious. He didn't really know what it was like to have a normal childhood. He was taught to work, to be serious, with little to no playtime. Now an adult himself, he realized that he had become just like his father. Those thoughts, those attitudes, those habits were what he had learned early on—not that they were right, but that's all he had known. Once he recognized what the source was, he was able to break that heaviness and really start enjoying his life.

CONSIDER THIS: Perhaps you have been spinning your wheels, going around in circles year after year, without really being happy. Understand, if you want to get to the source of the problem, you cannot just sit by idly and remain passive. You've got to come to the point where you say, "I am sick and tired of being sick and tired. I may have been this way for a long time, but I'm not going to dance around this issue. I'm going to get to the source, and I'm going to start making better decisions for my family and for me."

Take responsibility for your actions right now. Examine the negative history that is holding you back. Then in the space below, list ten positive steps you can take to break free of your negative actions. Maybe you need to seek a counselor. Maybe you need to talk to your pastor or confess to your spouse that you need help. Whatever it is, include it on the list below.

_____

_____

_____

_____

_____

_____

_____

_____

_____

_____

_____

_____

_____

_____   To exist is to change,
                                                  to change is to mature,
_____   to mature is to go on
                                              creating oneself endlessly.
_____

_____   —*Henri Bergson*

_____

_____

_____

_____

_____

_____

WHAT THE SCRIPTURES SAY

Do not conform any longer to the pattern of this world, but be transformed by the renewing of your mind. Then you will be able to test and approve what God's will is—his good, pleasing and perfect will.

—*Romans 12:2*

But the man who looks intently into the perfect law that gives freedom, and continues to do this, not forgetting what he has heard, but doing it—he will be blessed in what he does.

—*James 1:25*

A PRAYER FOR TODAY

God, show me what is keeping me from experiencing Your full blessing for me. Am I relying on other people to make me happy? Do I have unrealistic expectations? Am I allowing my circumstances to keep me down? Am I making excuses? God, show me the truth about myself.

Everybody thinks of changing humanity and nobody thinks of changing himself.

—Leo Tolstoy

TAKEAWAY TRUTH: I refuse to make excuses for myself; I will look inside and deal with the root, not simply the fruit. I will probe beyond the surface symptoms and get down to the source of my problems. I choose to overcome any unfair experiences by looking for the good God is bringing out of them.

STEP SEVEN

Stay Passionate About Life

DAY 1

PROVIDING FOR ABUNDANCE

KEY TRUTH: We have to go beyond believing. True faith puts action behind it.

There's an interesting story in the Bible about a widow. After her husband died she didn't have enough money to pay her bills. The creditors were coming to take her two sons as payment. The only thing she had of any value was a small pot of oil. Elisha the prophet showed up at her home and instructed her to do something rather unusual. He said, "Go out to all your neighbors and gather up as many large empty containers as you can find, big jars that can be used to hold oil." Elisha told her specifically, "Don't get just a few; get as many as you can possibly find."

No doubt it seemed like the woman was simply wasting her time. Elisha knew he had to get her faith going in the right direction. She had been sitting around long enough preparing for defeat. Now he was trying to get her to start preparing for victory. So she gathered up all sorts of empty containers, brought them home, and Elisha told her to pour the oil that she had into one of the other containers. At first, it looked like she was merely going to transfer it from one container to another, but the Scripture says her oil never ran out. She kept pouring and pouring and pouring. God supernaturally multiplied it until every single container was completely full. If she would have gotten a dozen more containers, they would gave been full as well.

The woman took a step of faith. It's not enough just to believe.

CONSIDER THIS: Friend, we are the ones who limit God; His resources are unlimited. If you will believe Him for more, regardless of your circumstances, He can provide—even if it takes a miracle to do so!

Let me challenge you. Have a big dream for your life. Make provision for abundance. In the space below, describe that dream—to get out of debt, to advance in your career, to send your kids to college, or whatever. Then list ten things you can do to make provision for that dream to come true.

All things are possible
until they are proved impossible—
and even the impossible
may only be so, as of now.

—*Pearl S. Buck*

_____

_____

_____

_____ ———⟨❧⟩———

_____ The only way of discovering
the limits of the possible
_____ is to venture a little way past
them into the impossible.
_____
—*Arthur C. Clarke*
_____

_____

_____

_____

_____

_____

_____

WHAT THE SCRIPTURES SAY

The Sovereign LORD is my strength;
he makes my feet like the feet of a deer,
he enables me to go on the heights.
　　　　　　—*Habakkuk 3:19*

Ask and it will be given to you; seek and you will find; knock and
the door will be opened to you. For everyone who asks receives; he
who seeks finds; and for him who knocks, the door will be opened.
　　　　　　　　　—*Luke 11:9–10*

A PRAYER FOR TODAY

Father, I thank You that right now You are working in my life. I thank You that right now I can plan for the blessings You have promised. And I thank You that by faith, through Your enabling, I'm getting better and better every day in every way.

_____

_____

_____

_____

_____

_____

_____

_____

_____

_____

_____

_____

_____

_____

TAKEAWAY TRUTH: This is going to be a blessed day. I'm going to have a good month. This is the best year of my life. I know great things are in store. Goodness and mercy are following me. God's favor is surrounding me. I am expecting increase, promotion, and abundance. I will prepare to succeed.

DAY 2

A SONG IN YOUR HEART

KEY TRUTH: God has put a well of joy inside of each one of us. If we can learn to tap into this joy, we can be happy, no matter what our circumstances are.

It's interesting how little children—even toddlers—become invigorated if you put on some good music. They start swaying, dancing, and clapping. The music energizes them. Interestingly, you don't have to teach them to do that. You don't have to say, "I'm about to turn on the music; get ready to move."

It comes naturally to them because God has put a song in their heart. In the same way, God has put rhythm in every one of us. Too often, we allow the pressures of life to weigh us down. We had this song when we were children. We were happy, carefree, excited about life. But over time, we've developed new habits: being sour, dragging through the day, not really being excited about life. We need to rediscover childlike faith, and when we do, we will also rediscover the song within us.

One day, our seven-year-old daughter, Alexandra, came in early in the morning. She was dressed and ready to go to school, so happy, so enthusiastic. She smiled real big and said, "Daddy, guess what? I've already sung two songs, and I've already done two cartwheels."

Victoria and I never asked Alexandra to sing. She just does. I can hear her all through the day. It's because God has put a song in her heart.

CONSIDER THIS: Throughout a day, no matter how filled we are at the start, we "leak" our happiness; we get pressured or stressed; life happens. You get stuck in traffic, and a little helium leaks out. You find out you didn't get the contract you were hoping for, and a little more escapes your balloon. You get home at the end of a hard day only to discover that your child is not feeling well and you must deal with the situation. The only way to stay full and to keep your joy and peace is to have a song of praise in your heart.

A song in your heart is not about music. It's an attitude. In our thoughts, we are grateful. We are excited about the future. We are expecting good things from God, so we allow a song to play continually in our minds. Reach deep into your heart, remembering all you are grateful to God for, and in the space below put words to the song in your heart. Let it spill out in whatever form it takes, like the irrepressible song of a bird in spring.

_____

_____

_____

_____

_____

_____

_____

_____

_____

_____

_____

_____   ⚬❈⚬

_____
                                        A bird does not sing
_____   because it has an answer.
                                     It sings because it has a song.
_____
                                          —*Chinese proverb*
_____
                                     _____

_____

_____

_____

_____

WHAT THE SCRIPTURES SAY

> Shout for joy to the LORD, all the earth,
> burst into jubilant song with music;
> make music to the LORD with the harp,
> with the harp and the sound of singing,
> with trumpets and the blast of the ram's horn—
> shout for joy before the LORD, the King.
> —*Psalm 98:4–6*

Speak to one another with psalms, hymns and spiritual songs. Sing and make music in your heart to the Lord, always giving thanks to God the Father for everything.
—*Ephesians 5:19–20*

A PRAYER FOR TODAY

God, I'm happy. God, I love You. I'm grateful to be alive. You are a shield to me, the glory and the lifter of my head. Hear the song in my heart, I pray, and accept my offering of praise, gratitude, and joy.

The hardest arithmetic
to master is that which enables
us to count our blessings.

—*Eric Hoffer*

TAKEAWAY TRUTH: Today, I will look for tangible ways that I can stay passionate about life. I will keep singing a song of joy in my heart, despite the circumstances. I will have a grateful attitude, recognizing that this day is a gift.

DAY 3

HOPE IS A SMILE

KEY TRUTH: If you'll smile by faith, soon the joy will follow.

God is concerned about your countenance. Fifty-three times in the Scripture, He mentions it. When you smile, it's not only good for yourself, but it's a good witness to others. They will want the sort of happiness that you have. It's one thing to talk about our faith, but it's a far better thing to live it out. One of the best witnesses we could ever have is simply to be happy, to have a smile, to be friendly and pleasant to be around.

Some people always seem to look as though they've lost their last friend. Even when they go to church, they look as though they were attending God's funeral!

Somebody asks, "How're you doing?"

"Oh, I'm just trying to hold on till Jesus comes," the starch-faced person replies.

No, we're not supposed to be merely holding on or dragging through life. Get your song back. Quit allowing the burdens of life to weigh you down. We all have tough times, hard things to handle, or heavy loads to carry. Don't allow your problems and circumstances to steal your joy.

Don't allow someone else to rob you of God's best. Too many people are being dragged down because somebody in their life is negative. Somebody else won't do right. Don't get into the pit with them. Keep your song.

CONSIDER THIS: You can choose what kind of song you're going to have. Don't be lazy in your thought life; speak to yourself in psalms and hymns. You talk to yourself throughout the day. Perhaps you have been talking to yourself in the wrong way.

Get your song back. Say things such as, "Father, thank You for this day. Thank You that I'm alive." Every time you do that, God will fill you afresh with His joy, His peace, His strength, His victory, and His favor. In the space below, write a letter to yourself, expressing the thoughts in your heart that produce a smile of joy and peace on your face.

_____

_____

_____

Hope smiles on the threshold
of the year to come,
whispering that it will
be happier.

—Alfred, Lord Tennyson

In every winter's heart there
is a quivering spring, and behind
the veil of each night there
is a smiling dawn.

—*Kahlil Gibran*

WHAT THE SCRIPTURES SAY

Then you will find your joy in the LORD,
and I will cause you to ride on the heights of the land
and to feast on the inheritance of your father Jacob.
　　　　　　　　　　　　　　—*Isaiah 58:14*

And we, who with unveiled faces all reflect the Lord's glory, are
being transformed into his likeness with ever-increasing glory.
　　　　　　　　　　　　　　—*2 Corinthians 3:18*

A PRAYER FOR TODAY

Lord, I know that when I keep my song and stay grateful it not only activates Your power, but it also replenishes me. It fills me up. So despite my circumstances, I choose to give You praise. I choose to thank You. I choose to smile as a witness of Your great love.

_____

_____

_____

_____

_____

_____

_____

_____

_____

_____

_____

_____

_____

_____

_____

_____

TAKEAWAY TRUTH: I'm not allowing another problem, another circumstance, or another person to keep me from giving God praise. I'm going to bless the Lord at all times. I'm going to get my song back.

DAY 4

PLAN FOR SUCCESS

KEY TRUTH: We have to wait on the Lord with expectancy.

I talked to Scott, a young man who has a dream to go to college. But nobody in his family has gone beyond high school. He immediately began listing all of his obstacles. "Joel, I don't know if I can afford it. I don't know if I'll make good enough grades. I don't know if they'll accept me. I don't know what my other family members will think." He was about to talk himself out of his dream.

Finally, I stopped him and said, "Scott, why don't you take a step of faith? Put some actions behind your prayers and at least fill out an application. Go tour the campus. Talk to the counselors. Make preparations to succeed. If you'll do what you can, then God will do what you can't."

Too often, we're believing one way, but our actions are demonstrating the opposite—we're actually preparing for defeat. Maybe you come from a long line of divorce in your family. Instead of being afraid of ever getting married or worrying that your marriage will end in divorce, you need to start planning what you're going to do on your first wedding anniversary, and on your fifth anniversary, and on your twenty-fifth anniversary. Speak words of vitality and life regarding your marriage. Don't say ". . . if we make it." Say ". . . *when* we make it!"

CONSIDER THIS: To wait with expectancy means that we are hopeful and positive. We get up every morning expecting good things. We may have problems, but we know this could be the day God turns it around. This could be the day I get the break that I need.

Waiting should not be a passive thing. Waiting the correct way means you are on the lookout. You talk as if what you believe is going to happen. You act as though it's going to happen. You are making preparations.

Which of God's promises are you waiting to come to pass? In the space below, list three expectations you have. Follow each with at least one action with which you are backing up your expectancy.

_____

_____

God gives every bird his worm,
but he does not throw it
into the nest.

—*Swedish proverb*

_____

_____

_____

_____

_____

_____

_____

_____

_____

_____

_____

_____   ———————⚮———————

_____   What great thing
                                        would you attempt
_____   if you knew you could
                                        not fail?
_____
                                        —*Robert H. Schuller*
_____
                                        ——————————————
_____

_____

_____

_____

_____

_____

WHAT THE SCRIPTURES SAY

Who through faith conquered kingdoms, administered justice, and gained what was promised; who shut the mouths of lions, quenched the fury of the flames, and escaped the edge of the sword; whose weakness was turned to strength . . .

—*Hebrews 11:33–34*

Faith, by itself, if it is not accompanied by action, is dead.

—*James 2:17*

A PRAYER FOR TODAY

God, I know You're in control, and I'm not going to be moved by doubt or despair. I know You are bigger than my obstacles. I believe at the right time, You will change things in my favor. By Your grace, I will stay my course, be courageous, and trust in You.

TAKEAWAY TRUTH: I choose to move from believing to expecting. Today I will reach for something beyond where I am presently. I will actively pursue new goals, keeping them out in front of me and expecting to meet them.

DAY 5

SAY NO TO NO

KEY TRUTH: Sometimes, to stay in faith, you must ignore a negative report.

John and Karen had become estranged from their son. Some things had happened, causing them to be at odds with each other. The young man wouldn't talk to his mother or father, wouldn't come visit them, wouldn't have anything to do with them. This went on month after month, until it looked as if they would never be reconciled.

But John and Karen refused to give up on their son. They took a step of faith and bought their son a Bible. They even had his name engraved on the front of it. The young man had never had anything to do with the things of God, so by all outward appearances, it seemed that his parents were wasting their money. They put the Bible on their coffee table anyway, and every time they walked by it, they thanked God that one day their son would be back home. One day, he would get back on the right course.

A few years later, they got a phone call from their son. "Mom and Dad," he said, "I want to come home." God supernaturally restored that relationship and today, I see that young man in church all the time, and he's carrying a Bible—but not just any

Bible. He's clutching that Bible with his name engraved on it, the same one that sat on that coffee table all those years.

John and Karen waited expectantly. They made preparations for their son to come back home, and today their entire family is reaping the benefits.

CONSIDER THIS: Sometimes people will try to talk you out of your dreams. Sometimes medical science will tell you there's nothing more they can do for you. Sometimes your own thoughts can even try to convince you of all the reasons why your dream, goal, or prayer request is not going to happen.

Start making preparations to live a blessed life. Keep your vision in front of you and don't believe the "never" lies: "I'll never get well." "I'll never see my dreams come to pass." No, shake that off, and stay positive and expectant. What are the "never" messages in your life right now? In the space below, write down five negative thoughts that are part of your present experience. Then after each one, turn it around to make a positive message that expects the positive and affirms God's plan to bless you.

_____

_____

_____

_____

_____

_____

_____

_____

_____

_____

_____

_____

_____

_____

_____

_____

_____

_____

_____

_____

_____

> Never doubt in the dark
> what God told you
> in the light.
> —*V. Raymond Edman*

WHAT THE SCRIPTURES SAY

Jesus did many other miraculous signs in the presence of his disciples, which are not written in this book. But these are written that you may believe that Jesus is the Christ, the Son of God, and that by believing you may have life in his name.

—John 20:30–31

Though now for a little while you may have had to suffer grief in all kinds of trials, these have come so that your faith—of greater worth than gold, which perishes even though refined by fire—may be proved genuine.

—1 Peter 1:6–7

A PRAYER FOR TODAY

God, my times are in Your hands. I don't know when it's going to happen, but I know You know what's best for me, so I'm going to expect good things. And even if it doesn't happen today, I'm not going to go to bed disappointed. I'll keep trusting that I am one day closer to seeing it come to pass.

Faith is building on what you know is here, so you can reach what you know is there.

—*Cullen Hightower*

TAKEAWAY TRUTH: I am waiting for the good things of God. I will learn to wait with expectancy. I'll get up every morning and thank God that the answer is on the way. I'll talk and act like it is going to happen. I know He will bring me the desires of my heart.

DAY 6

FANNING THE FLAME

KEY TRUTH: You need to quit looking at what's wrong in your life and start being grateful for what's right.

Understand that most of life is rather routine, and anything can become stagnant if we allow it to do so. You can have an exciting job, but it can become boring. Or you can be married to a fine, loving, caring person, but if you don't nourish that relationship and put something into it, over time, it is likely to get stagnant. We have to work at it if we're going to stay fresh. It doesn't automatically happen. We need to stir ourselves up every day.

Maybe today you are having difficulty being excited about your life, but keep your hope alive. You may have just a tiny flicker, and that fire is barely burning. You're about to give up on one of your dreams. Or maybe that relationship—you're not excited about it anymore. But the good news is the fire is still in there, and if you will do your part to fan the flame, it can burst forth into passion once again. That means instead of dragging around finding every reason you can to be unhappy, you must change your focus.

We need to recognize that every day is a gift from God. What a shame to live any day in a negative and defeated mind-set. You need to change your perspective. "I don't have to go to work today; I get to go to work." "I don't have to take care of these children, they're a blessing, I get to take care of them." "I don't have to give; I get to give."

CONSIDER THIS: Everything may not be perfect in your life, but if you don't learn to be happy where you are, you will never get to where you want to be. Understand that it dishonors God to go around complaining and thinking about everything that's wrong in your life. When those negative, discouraging thoughts come, you must turn them around. Fan your passion with fresh goals. After you accomplish a goal, immediately set another.

What are you looking forward to today, this week, this month, this year? What have you set for yourself to accomplish? In the space below, write down five things you're grateful for, five things you're looking forward to, and five goals. That's five, five, and five. Be specific and realistic.

Life is not a "brief candle."
It is a splendid torch
that I want to make burn
as brightly as possible
before handing it on to
future generations.

—*Bernard Shaw*

_____

_____

_____

_____

_____   —⟨∞⟩—

_____   If we live good lives,
                             the times are also good.
_____   As we are, such are the times.

_____   —*St. Augustine*

_____

_____   _____

_____

_____

_____

_____

_____

_____

WHAT THE SCRIPTURES SAY

Be joyful always; pray continually; give thanks in all circumstances, for this is God's will for you in Christ Jesus. Do not put out the Spirit's fire.

—*1 Thessalonians 5:16–19*

I remind you to fan into flame the gift of God, which is in you through the laying on of my hands.

—*2 Timothy 1:6*

A PRAYER FOR TODAY

Lord, You have blessed me with so many gifts, I can't even count them. You have given me breath and life and great opportunities. Provide me with the vision and the stamina, I pray, to make the most of this day and give it my best.

_____

_____

_____

_____

_____

_____

_____

_____

_____

_____

_____

_____

_____

_____

TAKEAWAY TRUTH: I am not going to live my life defeated and depressed. My dreams may not have come to pass yet; I may have some obstacles in my path, but I know God is still in control. I know He's got great things in store for me, so I'm going to get up each day excited about my life.

DAY 7

WILLING WHAT'S RIGHT

KEY TRUTH: When you do the right thing with the right motives, there's no limit to what God will do in your life.

Years ago, my father and I met Jacques Cousteau, the famous underwater explorer. Daddy and I were on a flight down to the Amazon jungle and Mr. Cousteau was on the same flight, so we engaged in conversation. He was probably in his early eighties, yet he was incredibly passionate about his life. He began telling us about a new project he was working on, excitedly explaining it in great detail. As we were about to leave, he told us about his ten-year plan and all that he hoped to accomplish. I thought, *Most people his age are not thinking ahead much more than a week or a month. But Jacques Cousteau is still thinking ten years down the road.* No wonder he was so vibrantly alive.

My dad kept a globe everywhere he worked—at his chair at home where he studied and on his desk at the office. Daddy's passion was to share God's love all over the world, and that globe reminded him of that. Even later in my father's life when he had to go on dialysis, he asked us to check to see if they could do dialysis in India. Although Daddy never made it back to India once he started dialysis, that didn't keep him from dreaming. In fact, that was one of the things that helped him to get up every day with enthusiasm in spite of his adversity.

CONSIDER THIS: If you really want to experience God's best, you need to be more than obedient; you have to be willing. You have to do the right thing with the right attitude.

For instance, it's one thing to give because you have to. It's another thing to give because you want to. It's one thing to go to work to pick up the paycheck. It's another thing to go to work to be a blessing to somebody else. It's one thing to stay married to that person because it's the right thing to do. People may look down on you if you don't. But it's another thing to stay married to that person and to treat him or her with respect and honor and help your partner reach a higher level. That's being willing and obedient. It's important that we get beyond mere obedience. That's easy, anybody can do that. To become a better you, take the next step and be willing to do the right thing with a good attitude. Write out ten ways in which you are obedient to God's calling in your life. When you've finished, write a paragraph describing the attitude that raises that obedience to a higher level of enthusiasm, passion, and commitment. For every "what," you should be able to give a worthy "why."

_____

_____

_____

_____

_____

_____

_____

_____

_____
_____
_____
_____
_____   ————————— ❧ —————————
_____
_____   I still find each day too short
_____   for all the thoughts I want to
_____   think, all the walks I want
_____   to take, all the books I want to
_____   read, and all the friends
_____   I want to see.
_____
_____   *—John Burroughs*
_____   _____

_____
_____
_____
_____
_____

WHAT THE SCRIPTURES SAY

If you are willing and obedient,
you will eat the best from the land.
          —Isaiah 1:19

No eye has seen,
no ear has heard,
no mind has conceived
what God has prepared for those who love him.
          —1 Corinthians 2:9

A PRAYER FOR TODAY

Father, I pray that You will give me a spirit of gratitude that focuses on the good and never takes it for granted. Help me to trust You each day and live according to Your plan for my life. Fill me with Your joy and keep me on the path to the greatness You have in mind for me.

_____

_____

_____

_____

Look at everything   _____
as though you were seeing it
either for the first or last time.   _____
Then your time on earth
will be filled with glory.   _____

—Betty Smith   _____

                                         _____

_____

_____

_____

TAKEAWAY TRUTH: Today is unique and irreplaceable. I will make the most of it, and live like it could be my last. First thing every day I will set my mind in the right direction for success and victory.